Drying Silent Tears

GARRY JAMES

Foreword by Dr. R.T. Kendall

Drying Silent Tears
Copyright © 2009 by Garry James
Published by KLS/LifeChange.

Dewey Decimal Classification: 362.76
Subject Heading: Children, Abuse and Neglect, Counseling

Library of Congress Cataloging-in-Publication Data

James, Garry, 1963–
       Drying Silent Tears, Garry James, 2009
          p. cm.
       Includes bibliographic references.

       ISBN– 978-0-9648743-9-8

1. Christian life–Parenting 2. Child Abuse.

For more information contact:
Garry James
www.dryingsilenttears.org
www.castinc.org

Unless otherwise indicated, all Scripture quotations are taken from The Holy Bible, New King James Version. Copyright © 1982 by Thomas Nelson, Inc. Used by permission of Thomas Nelson, Inc.

Verses marked Phillips are taken from J.B. Phillips: The New Testament in Modern English. (D 1958, 1960.) Used by permission of Macmillan Publishing Company.

Contents

Foreword

Please read this book. If you do, you will hardly be the same again. If, however, you are like me, you will be shocked and awakened by the information that awaits you. I myself was brought up in a Christian home filled with love and care. I knew nothing of the sort of thing this book describes. It made me so thankful for having parents like I had. I realize more than ever how I have taken this privilege too much for granted. If you are like me, you will be introduced to a world filled with evil and perverseness that you had not been aware of.

Many of us have seen horrifying pictures of starving children with their swollen stomachs in Third World countries such as Africa. But how many of us are conscious of children right under our noses, living in our own neighborhoods, who are suffering an unthinkable horror because of ruthless authority figures who take advantage of them. This book addresses the issue of child abuse and neglect in a scholarly, theological, but readable manner and provides the best way forward I can think of to deal with what I can only call an epidemic. The information you will receive from reading this book will not provide a pretty picture, but you will be so glad that someone has done the research and has the vision to see accomplished what is long overdue. Nobody can do everything, and each of us has our own gift and calling. I am just glad that God has raised up the author of this book to write on a subject I have known so little about. He wants the church to become an involved church in a fallen world. In this valuable and timely book Dr. James shows what you and I can do in a practical way to help.

Dr. Garry James is a pastor in the southern part of the United States of America. My wife and I have known Dr. James and his wife for over six years. The book you hold in your hands was originally written as his Doctor of Ministry thesis and has been slightly edited for a wider distribution without forfeiting the knowledge and careful research that lies behind his burden. His burden is to see the Church generally and Christians particularly (1) awakened to see the growing issue of child abuse and neglect, (2) become aware of how wrong people are moving in and exploiting vulnerable situations and (3) how Christians can get involved to provide help.

This book could be used to discover, prepare, and preserve future leaders and citizens that will turn tomorrow's world upside down. I shudder to think of how many children are growing up with such a bleak future in a country that has been so enriched. This book could be the tool that could snatch children from a hell on earth to give them a bit of heaven below.

Dr. R.T. Kendall
Former Minister, Westminster Chapel, London, England
June 23, 2008

Dedication

This book is dedicated to the millions of children that have been victimized by child maltreatment. It is also dedicated to the countless number of adults that continue to harbor pain from incidents of abuse and neglect that occurred during their childhood. May the Lord of hosts heal your pain and guide you into a bright future.

Author's Preface

The most precious gift of all is the gift of life. The privilege of working in the area of children's services for a number of years reminds me daily that many people are robbed of this gift. Even more remarkable is the fact that there is not a more concerted effort being made by members of our society to seek solutions for this enormous problem. The last position that I held in the area of children's services was as a trainer in the staff development and training division of the Department of Social Services. My professional career had come full circle as I had an opportunity to train front line child protective services social workers. Our staff sought to equip these newly hired professionals with the wisdom and knowledge gained from serving in the field for a number of years.

My co-worker, Mary Landrum, thoroughly enjoyed sharing our combined forty plus years of experience with the new and energetic social workers who were seeking to make a difference in the lives of the children and families whom they served. However, throughout our years in the training division both Mary and I realized that something was missing. We knew that there was an essential dynamic that was not a part of the curriculum that was vital to addressing the needs of our clients. The fact that we were employees of our state restricted us from venturing into the spiritual dynamics associated with the maltreatment of children. We were unable share in great detail how biblical principles were needed to provide fundamental solutions for an epidemic that is traditionally handled with secular methods.

This book is the outcome of a discussion that Ms. Landrum and I had one afternoon as we pondered–what if? Our world is in desperate need of practical solutions to a problem that transcends gender, ethnicity, social class, and religion. Consider making the journey with me to be a part of the solution.

Introduction

There is a good chance that you have begun reading this book by the divine providence of God. We know that the Lord never makes mistakes and His plans and timing are impeccable. It is my prayer that as you apprehend the content of the following chapters you will discover a world that lies beneath the surface of mainstream society. In this world you will find an epidemic of child abuse and neglect that has existed for thousands of years. Most are unaware of the vastness of the problem. From time to time we hear of occurrences within our communities but these incidents represent only a small percentage of what is taking place daily within our neighborhoods.

As with any problem the Lord always provides answers. I feel that the vision for this text was given to me for providing solutions that will empower you as you begin to understand and apply biblical principles that can help reduce the frequency of child abuse and neglect. Whenever an illness is diagnosed the most effective remedies are those that address the root cause. The following chapters not only uncover the root cause but provide God's answers to effectively engage the issue. It is a tool that can be used to educate and empower parents, teachers, school administrators, social workers, caregivers, and anyone who has a desire to protect children. It can also be used to provide an avenue for healing and restoration for those children and adults that have been affected.

Triumphs as well as defeats, victories and also valleys, hope and the reality that we must become involved in addressing the constant threat of harm looming over all children are provided here. This book exists to provide an opportunity for people to begin to understand the dynamics of child maltreatment. It also can enlighten the body of Christ by illustrating how we can effectively overcome pandemic problems in our world by becoming an involved church.

As you read this book, begin putting the principles into practice. May the Lord God Almighty receive all of the glory as your efforts provide a safe haven for His little ones. I pray the Lord will give you direction for those who have been harmed as you introduce them to the Great Physician.

Chapter One
An Unthinkable History

Ellen recalls being physically abused by her mother around the age of five. Memories still linger of lying on the upper level of her bunk bed when her mother suddenly roared into her bedroom, grabbed her by the hair, and threw her to the floor. Her mother kicked her repeatedly as Ellen tumbled out of the bedroom and down the hallway. The abusive episode ended as she was thrown down a flight of stairs. Ellen questioned what she could have done to make her mother so angry. She frantically tried to replay the events of the past few days to see if there was anything she had done that could have possibly justified this type of punishment. Nothing came to mind.

The next violent outburst occurred when Ellen returned from a visit to the local hospital after sustaining an injury. Her mother erupted into an unprovoked tirade, slamming Ellen's head into the bathroom sink, splitting her head open and leaving permanent scars on her scalp. The situation at home only worsened when Ellen's parents separated and later divorced. Unfortunately, she became the primary focus of her mother's anger. Ellen felt that anything she tried to accomplish would provoke her mother and result in her being physically abused.

Ellen continued to struggle with various emotional and social issues that hindered her ability to enjoy life. Countless others have transitioned from childhood into adulthood with excess emotional stress because of an abusive past. The difficulties Ellen faced stemmed from her abusive childhood. Her story reflects the brutal reality faced daily by thousands of children. Not only are many of them tormented by physical abuse, they are also subjected to other forms of abuse and neglect. An overview of Ellen's experience offers valuable insight and allows entry into the world of the abused and neglected child. Her story lends support to those who continue to struggle because of an abusive past and offers them encouragement to discover the biblical remedy for child abuse and neglect. Christian involvement in the battle against child abuse and neglect is critical.

As Ellen matured into adulthood she confronted memories of being beaten for misspelling words on her homework assignment, while at other times having poisonous household cleanser poured on her hands for not being the perfect child. As she entered the fourth grade the physical abuse was coupled with mental and emotional insults. Her mother began to focus on her imperfections more than on any of her accomplishments. The insults ranged from being criticized as the most unattractive fourth grader in town to belittling comparisons between "bad" Ellen and the "good" children in the neighborhood. The physical and emotional anguish faced by Ellen during her childhood was more than any human should have to endure. Unfortunately, many children do not survive their abuse to tell their story. Fortunately for Ellen, and for every child and adult who does survive, there is a bright ray of sunshine and hope at the end of their dark tunnel.

As Bright As The Son

Through all of the pain and suffering Ellen held one hope close to her heart. This glimmer of sunshine allowed her to survive her childhood abuse. Simple and yet profound, her saving grace was knowing that God was nearby and that she could talk to Him whenever she desired. Her simple childlike faith in the LORD and the practical application of His Word brought true healing. Faith gave her the strength to endure, and ultimately overcome the physical, mental, and emotional pain associated with the harsh treatment from her mother. Although there were other negative experiences in her childhood, Ellen's belief in God allowed her to conquer the trauma of her formative years and become a productive adult with a passion to love and serve others. Like Ellen, those who have experienced traumatic childhoods have a myriad of memories and, often times, physical reminders that make life difficult to navigate. Regardless of the difficulties in life, the LORD is more than willing to provide healing and restoration in the life of anyone who gives Him the opportunity.

The Enormity of the Problem

National statistics collected annually by the *United States Department of Health and Human Services* reflect that there are over 740,517 substantiated cases of child abuse and neglect (known hereafter as child maltreatment) in the United States alone.[1] Statisticians have reported that this data reveals only a portion of the actual number of children who are being maltreated in America. *Child Protective Services* confirms that there are many screened out reports. Many are because of what social workers and law enforcement officials call a preponderance of evidence. This simply implies that there is not enough evidence to substantiate the report as being true. The fact that many reports are screened out because of a lack of evidence does not mean a crime did not occur. Also, many of these crimes are never reported to *Child Protective Services* in an effort to protect the child and/or the guilty party. Consequently, many unknown abused children need to be discovered and given that same glimmer of sunshine that Ellen embraced as a child.

The United States is arguably the last remaining super power in the world. There still remain issues within its communities that have yet to be addressed with the necessary strategies and resources needed to eradicate problems, such as the frequent occurrences of child maltreatment. While the number of cases of abuse and neglect in America is astounding, one can only imagine how these numbers pale in comparison to those of other countries that are not being policed and/or monitored as stringently as the United States. Accounts of international incidents of child maltreatment are regularly broadcast through local and national media. The *International Justice Mission* made it their aim to bring attention to these travesties that occur daily. Governing authorities in other countries are often made aware of these crimes but do not act upon the reports for various reasons. Children in these countries are not afforded the opportunity of being reared in a safe and nurturing environment. They are beaten, neglected, sold into prostitution, and made to work in conditions that are not fit for humans. Why then have the necessary steps been avoided to decrease the national numbers of abuse and neglect? One of the reasons is the process of desensitization.

Desensitizing the Pain

The frequent reporting of child maltreatment by the global media has desensitized viewers and listeners alike to the tremendous pain associated with each occurrence of child maltreatment. Overwhelming incidents being reported has seared people's consciences, resulting in apathy and complacency. Public outrage regarding stories of child maltreatment used to be the norm. Now, cries for justice have become little more than sterile whimpers as the human mind has become saturated to a point of indifference. Consequently, callous walls have developed in the hearts of some of the world's best citizens because of the process of desensitization. Neil Postman writes:

The viewers also know that no matter how grave any fragment of news may appear (for example, on the day I write a Marine Corps general has declared that nuclear war between the United States and Russia is inevitable), it will shortly be followed by a series of commercials that will, in an instant, defuse the importance of the news, in fact render it largely banal...We have become so accustomed to its discontinuities that we are no longer struck dumb, as any sane person would be, by a newscaster who having just reported that a nuclear war is inevitable goes on to say that he will be right back after this word from Burger King...The damage is especially massive to youthful viewers who depend so much on television for their clues as to how to respond to the world.[2]

Even skilled social workers that have accepted the challenge to combat child maltreatment have to continually be on guard so that they do not minimize the trauma experienced by the children and the families they serve. If social workers are not careful, the children they vow to protect become little more than "products" in a massive assembly line. Human services management must be more concerned with the genuine care of their clients than with their agency's financial bottom line.

Society must revisit the vision and mission of combating the sin of child maltreatment, rethink the amount and distribution of resources, strengthen local and national governmental legislation against perpetrators, and aggressively pursue global accountability. With that in mind, these "musts" merely address the symptoms of a much more deeply rooted problem.

Both Christian and secular counselors agree that in order to effectively resolve problems that their clients face, they must be able to assist them in the discovery of the root cause of their pain.[3] This discovery allows them to begin the healing process. In order to effectively resolve the issue of child maltreatment, the root cause, not merely the symptoms of this sin issue, must be discovered and effectively confronted. The discovery of the root cause is starting point for effective and efficient healing. To accomplish this task, members of society can no longer allow themselves to become desensitized to a point of indifference. They must discover and confront the root cause of the problem. As with all dysfunctions in our world, the genesis of child maltreatment can be discovered by revisiting the biblical events surrounding Adam and Eve in the Garden of Eden.

The Root Cause of Child Abuse & Neglect

Scripture attributes the beginning of humanity's sinful nature to the events that took place in the Garden of Eden described in Genesis 2-3. The spiritual fall of man was the result of Adam and Eve's rebellious decision to disobey the LORD's commandments. Eating fruit from the tree of knowledge of good and evil was their act of disobedience. As a result of this initial sin, Christian theologians have correctly declared that all of mankind sinned corporately in Adam. This sinful condition can be only be remedied by individuals accepting the LORD Jesus Christ as their personal Savior. As a result of sin entering into the world through Adam, man continues to struggle with sin. Child abuse and neglect is one significant way that sin affected children's lives.

The maltreatment of children cannot be comfortably tucked away under a medical or psychological diagnosis, nor can it be hidden under the guise of a cultural tradition. Child abuse and neglect is sin and an abomination against God. It is a crime against the most vulnerable members of the human race. Sin is the root cause of child maltreatment. According to Scripture, the only effective remedy for sin is genuine repentance. Henry Brandt and Kerry Skinner state, "Repentance is a five-step process involving God and you. In God's presence you must personally profess: (1) I am wrong; I have sinned. (2) I am sorry. (3) Forgive me. (4) Cleanse me. (5)

Empower me."[4] Without acknowledging sin and embracing the only remedy for sin (genuine repentance), the foundational strategy to resolve child maltreatment is missing an essential element that hinders its effectiveness. The issue of sin and repentance will be discussed in chapters related to healing (chapter 5) and perpetrators (chapter 8) of child maltreatment.

Where It All Began

The earliest recorded accounts of child maltreatment occurred generations before the birth of Jesus Christ. Scriptural evidence reveals many instances of child abuse occurring in the first book of the Bible. In Genesis 12:2-3 the LORD called Abram out of his homeland and into another place where he said, "I will bless you and make your name great; and you shall be a blessing...and in you all the families of the earth shall be blessed." However, there were specific relational conditions concerning the native inhabitants of the land promised to Abram. The conditions were simple, direct, and not in need of further revelation. Abram was instructed not to mingle with the people that inhabited the Promised Land. Adam had a similar command given to him by God. Adam had the privilege of enjoying all the fruit from every tree in the Garden except for one. Abraham, like Adam, was able to enjoy all that the land had to offer, for it was "a good and large land, to a land flowing with milk and honey." However, the LORD prohibited His people from mingling or marrying the natives and from worshipping the idols of the land.

The LORD even instructed the Israelites to destroy the current occupants (Deut. 20:17). Without a proper understanding of the worship and ritualistic practices of the inhabitants of the Promised Land, God's instructions would appear severe, even heartless. God knew what Abraham and the Israelites did not know about those who lived in Canaan. God knew that their practices included the slaughtering of innocent children. Sinful man's fallen nature became evident through the ritualistic sacrificial offering of children to idols made of wood, stone, silver, and gold–all in the name of religious worship.

Abraham instructed his chief servant not to let his son Isaac choose a bride from the daughters of the Canaanites (Gen. 24:2-4). Isaac followed the obedience modeled by Abraham, and did not intermingle with the Canaanites. Isaac also instructed his son Jacob to obey the commandments of the LORD (Gen. 28:1). Jacob, likewise, was obedient to the commandments of the LORD as he followed the path chosen by his grandfather, Abraham, and his father, Isaac. It is ironic that the LORD, who in Genesis 22 tested Abraham's faith by asking him to offer Isaac as a sacrifice (yet would not allow the act to occur), chose Abraham and Isaac as conduits of His instructions to protect children. Abraham, Isaac, and Jacob are considered righteous men of the Christian faith, for they obeyed the instructions of the LORD and did not mingle with those that occupied the Promised Land. However, Jacob's twin brother, Esau, disobeyed the commands of both his heavenly and earthly fathers and married not one but three wives from the land of Canaan (Gen. 36:2-5). One of Jacob's twelve sons, Judah, also disobeyed God, as he also married a Canaanite. Scripture declares, "And Judah saw there a daughter of a certain Canaanite whose name was Shua, and he married her and went in to her." The disobedience of Esau and Judah served as a spark that began the fire of intimate mingling with the Canaanites. Accepting a Canaanite wife led to accepting her sacrificial practices.

In his book *Canaanites: Peoples of the Past,* Jonathan Tubb writes, "as far as the practice of the cult is concerned, the Ugaritic texts make it clear that Canaanite religion was a religion of blood sacrifice."[5] John Day provides further evidence of the grisly sacrificial practices of the Canaanites, stating, "since antiquity, references in the Hebrew Scriptures and remarks in ancient Greek and Roman authors have been cited to prove that various Northwest Semitic peoples practiced child sacrifice."[6] Additional evidence of child exploitation is found in the writings of Shelby Brown. In reference to the various Northern Semetic peoples that Day referenced, Brown states, "these include the population whom the Hebrew Scriptures call Canaanites; the people whom modern scholars, following the Greeks, call Phoenicians; and Phoenicians who settled in the western Mediterranean and whom modern scholars, following the Romans call Punic. In fact, at the sites of Punic settlements have been found burial grounds that contain the cremated remains only of young children and animals. Archaeologists call such burial grounds *tophets* after the Hebrew term for the place where children were sacrificed."[7]

A tragedy is described in 2 Kings as the Moabite king Mesha performs an act of desperation in response to an onslaught by the army of Israel. As the Israelite army advanced against his troops, Scripture reveals the following:

> Then they [the Israelites] destroyed the cities, and each man threw a stone on every good piece of land and filled it; and they stopped up all the springs of water and cut down all the good trees. But they left the stones of Kir Haraseth intact. However the slingers surrounded and attacked it. And when the king of Moab saw that the battle was too fierce for him, he took with him seven hundred men who drew swords, to break through to the king of Edom, but they could not. Then he took his eldest son who would have reigned in his place, and offered him as a burnt offering upon the wall; and there was great indignation against Israel. So they departed from him and returned to their own land.
>
> 2 Kings 3:25-27

This ghastly passage, along with the aforementioned archaeological evidence, illustrates a distinct pattern of child maltreatment in the Old Testament. It is difficult to refute biblical, archaeological, and scholarly evidence that clearly establishes that the original inhabitants of the Promised Land did indeed engage in ritualistic child sacrifices. Whenever man continually disobeys the commands of the LORD, the only possible outcome will be that of immoral, ungodly behavior resulting in dreadful consequences.

Sacrificing to Baal & Lesser gods

Since it has been determined that the origin of child maltreatment dates back to the Old Testament, the primary source of these crimes should be revealed in order to effectively address the sin. Leviticus 18:21 assists in the identification of the primary perpetrators of child maltreatment as the LORD spoke the following words to Moses: "And you shall not let any of your descendants pass through the fire to Molech, nor shall you profane the name of your God: I am the LORD." This passage provides biblical evidence that children were being offered as sacrifices to a god by the name of Molech. God, having all knowledge, knew of the sacrificial practices of the original inhabitants of Canaan. The LORD certainly did not want the children of Israel to be influenced by nor to ultimately embrace the sins of their culture.

There were several sacrificial forms of child maltreatment discovered that were associated with the worship of the false god Molech. According to Bob Boyd, "it is evident from the pick and spade of the archaeologist that human sacrifices were made to Baal and to some of the lesser gods."[8] Boyd continues, "the sacrificing of children was done sometimes by a priest who would carve the child with a sharp knife, placing the parts of the body on an altar with fire underneath, and offering this to Baal as a burnt-offering."[9] The second method took place at sites called the Fires of Molech. Baal worshippers would construct idols out of brass, fashioning the face in the likeness of an ox or that of a calf. The brass idol would then be heated until red-hot. Children were then placed on the searing idol and their bodies were consumed by roaring flames in an effort to appease the god Molech. During these ceremonies other priests would beat drums called *tophets* to drown out the sounds of crying children and their mothers. The Hebrew word *tophet* became synonymous with the terms drum or a place of fire. The rationale for the drums was to prevent the fathers from hearing the cries of their family members, since they would have been moved with sympathy and compassion to put an end to the murdering of innocent children.

In similar ceremonies, some children were made to take a "walk of death" through rows of Molechs where several of these brass idols were heated to such high temperatures that the children would expire in the midst of them. Those that sacrificed children to Molech did so believing that by offering their children to this god, they would somehow secure good fortune for themselves and their families.

Lloyd deMause, the director of the *Institute for Psychohistory*, has dedicated over three decades of his life to conducting research on the maltreatment of children throughout the course of history. According to deMause,

> A typical child sacrifice for parental success can be seen in Carthage, where archaeologists have found a child cemetery called the Tophet that is filled with 20,000 urns containing bones of children sacrificed by the parents, who would make a vow to kill their next child if the gods would grant them a favor–for instance, if their shipment of goods were to arrive safely in a foreign port.[10]

A total disregard for human life coupled with self-centered motives served as the impetus for the sacrificial murders of children in order to gain the favor of false gods. Other archaeological and historical evidence provides proof of child maltreatment in that era.

Other Sacrificial Practices

Joseph Free made a startling discovery of other errant practices during an archaeological dig at the Old Testament site of Dothan. While participating in the excavation of Dothan, the excavation team discovered the skeletal remains of an infant. The ceremonially dressed child was found underneath the foundation of a wall within the city. Historians have noted that during this period infants were sometimes placed in the foundations of important buildings or walls of cities as consecration sacrifices to gods. Similar to the beliefs of others during that period, it was felt that good fortune would be obtained by those who were willing to murder their young. Those conducting the excavation uncovered extensive ceremonial garb on the infant skeletons, including bracelets for wrists and ankles.[11]

Nigel Davies described other accounts of senseless violence against children that occurred among the Carthaginians. Davies reports that the Carthaginians "specialized" in child sacrifices and "inherited these practices from their Phoenician and Canaanite ancestors."[12] Reports illustrate that the atrocities committed by the Baal worshippers of Carthage occurred for the sole purposes of psychic revelation. During ceremonies to false gods, Baal worshippers used the entrails of children to determine what the future might hold for them and their families.

The Romans, who destroyed and later rebuilt Carthage, gradually adopted similar practices of abuse. Roman culture was driven by materialism, luxury, and self-centered behavior. Emperors such as Caligula and Nero lived extravagant lives, and their wicked practices included the sexual abuse of boys.

Confusion in Christianity

The consequences of Christian disobedience are documented throughout Scripture and other historical records. However, far too little attention has been given to the results of Israel's disobedience when they rebelled against the LORD and adopted the sacrificial customs of the Canaanites. The prophet Ezekiel provides an Old Testament perspective on the evil actions exhibited by those early Israelites as well as giving God's response:

> For they have committed adultery, and blood is on their hands. They have committed adultery with their idols, and even sacrificed their sons whom they bore to Me, passing them through the fire, to devour them. Moreover they have done this to Me: They have defiled My sanctuary on the same day and profaned My Sabbaths. For after they had slain their children for their idols, on the same day they came into My sanctuary to profane it; and indeed thus they have done in the midst of My house.

> Ezekiel 23:37–39

At first glance the language of these passages appears to refer to pagans such as the Canaanites, who exhibited a corrupt and foul lifestyle. However, careful examination of the Scriptures reveals that the LORD is speaking through Ezekiel regarding the ungodly behavior of the children of Israel. Having failed to follow the instructions of the LORD concerning the Canaanites, the children of Israel began to embrace the ungodly ritualistic practices of the original inhabitants of Canaan.

King Solomon, one of the most recognizable and successful biblical figures in the Old Testament, fell prey to this ungodly influence as well. Christians are taught from childhood about the great exploits of King Solomon, and rightfully so. The life of Solomon engenders many quality character traits that should be modeled by Christians. One example is when King Solomon voiced a humble prayer for wisdom in 1 Kings 3:6-9. This passage provides a phenomenal leadership trait: humble admission of his dependence upon the LORD for wisdom. However, along with his many positive attributes, Solomon displayed some behavioral traits that did not coincide with the will of God. He became so captivated by the ungodly practices of his many wives and concubines that he adopted their ritualistic practices. 1 Kings 11:1-2 provides scriptural evidence that implicates Solomon's involvement in child abuse.

> But King Solomon loved many foreign women, as well as the daughter of Pharaoh: women of the Moabites, Ammonites, Edomites, Sidonians, and Hittites—from the nations of whom the LORD had said to the children of Israel, "You shall not intermarry with them, nor they with you. Surely they will turn away your hearts after their gods." Solomon clung to these in love.

Solomon, like Esau and Judah, disobeyed the will of God and took wives from those tribes that served Baal. This resulted in Solomon embracing the sacrificial practices of his wives and concubines. Davies provides a summary that captures the true essence of both Solomon's and Israel's sin relative to child maltreatment.

> The cult of these foreign deities was once so widespread among the Israelites that even Solomon (973–933 B.C.) succumbed. His hundred wives "turned his heart after other gods." He raised a high place within sight of Jerusalem to Chemosh, the Moabite form of Baal in whose honour Mesha had burned his son and heir, and also built a temple to Moloch.[13]

In Romans 6:23 the apostle Paul writes that, "the wages of sin is death." Although this passage refers to a spiritual death that leads to eternal damnation, in the case of Israel's disobedience, their defiance of the commands of the LORD led to the literal physical death of many children. What could possibly prompt those that had a heart for the LORD to be led down a slippery homicidal slope?

The Main Perpetrator

The primary focus of any investigation of child maltreatment is to locate and prosecute the human perpetrators of the crimes. The main perpetrator in any case of abuse and neglect cannot be seen with the human eye. Yet, the aftermath of his influence is extremely visible and is manifested before the world. It is as devastating as a natural disaster that has wreaked havoc in the lives of millions. Psalm 106 sheds light on the ultimate perpetrator of all of the pain and suffering associated with child maltreatment:

> They also provoked Him to wrath at the waters of Meribah, So that it went hard with Moses on their account; because they were rebellious against His Spirit, He spoke rashly with his lips. They did not destroy the peoples, as the LORD commanded them, but they mingled with the nations and learned practices, and served their idols, which became a snare to them. They even sacrificed their sons and their daughters to the demons, and shed innocent blood, the blood of their sons and their daughters, whom they sacrificed to the idols of Canaan; and the land was polluted with the blood.

Psalm 106:32–38

The Psalmist wrote that children were being sacrificed to demons. Scripture recognizes sacrifices to Molech, Ashteroth, and Baal. The Psalmist correctly differentiates sacrifices as being made to demons, not merely to false gods. Most in contemporary society affiliate child maltreatment with evil, and rightfully so. However true this may be, citizens in the twenty-first century should be both candid and forthright when identifying the true source. These acts are not merely evil but are associated with Satan and his demonic legion of fallen angels. Those who participate in this ritualistic idolatry are not associated merely with a type of cultural evil but with demonic rulers, authorities, principalities, and powers. Paul writes in Ephesians 6:12: "For our struggle is not against flesh and blood, but against the rulers, against the authorities, against the powers of this dark world and against the spiritual forces of evil in the heavenly realms."

The main perpetrators of child maltreatment are not those people who murder, neglect, physically injure, or sexually abuse children. Those that carry out these despicable acts are responsible for their decisions and should face the maximum consequences for their crimes. However, the ultimate perpetrators are hidden behind the scenes of these criminal incidents. The passage in Ephesians reveals them as wicked spiritual beings, recognized as fallen angels. Satan is the leader of this evil group and Scripture declares that his primary goal is to steal, kill, and to destroy (John 10:10).

Boyd shares insight into the reality of Ephesians 6 with regard to child maltreatment. Boyd writes, "Baal was often designated 'Zebul'–meaning Prince. Baal-zebub, god of the Ekronites (2 Kings 1:2), is a derivative of the name Baal-zebul."[14] In demonic worship, "Princely Baal" was the name for Satan, "Prince of Demons." Any biblical concordance will provide similar descriptions and scriptural references for the name closely related to Baal-zebub, namely Beelzebub. The words of the LORD Jesus Christ provide a clear linkage between the two in Luke 15:14-18:

> Jesus was driving out a demon that was mute. When the demon left, the man who had been mute spoke, and the crowd was amazed. But some of them said, "By Beelzebub, the prince of demons, he is driving out demons." Others tested him by asking for a sign from heaven. Jesus knew their thoughts and said to them: 'Any kingdom divided against itself will be ruined, and a house divided against itself will fall. If Satan is divided against himself, how can his kingdom stand?

The source of all forms of evil is identified by name in this passage; namely, Beelzebub, or as identified by Christ in Luke 15, Satan.

The importance of properly recognizing the source of child maltreatment is paramount in developing solutions to the problem. If a physician treats the symptoms of an illness and never addresses the root cause then that individual would not be providing what those in the medical profession term "best practice." The same applies to effectively resolving child maltreatment. Historically, treatment has centered on dealing with the symptoms of abuse and neglect without the root cause having been addressed. Chapter 5, titled "Heal Me LORD," provides an in-depth discussion for those who have been subject to abuse and neglect as well as for those who have been the perpetrators of child maltreatment. The biblical approach taken in this chapter will provide what the LORD considers "best practice" for dealing with Satan, who is the root cause and main perpetrator of the social pariah known as child maltreatment.

The Progression of child maltreatment

With recent advancements in education, technology, transportation, and communication, humanity can consider itself truly blessed of God. The LORD has exponentially increased man's knowledge over the last one hundred years. God has given him the capacity to resolve complex problems, to establish dynamic methodologies in many areas, and to develop life-changing technologies. These progressions have occurred at a higher rate than at any other period of time in the history of the world. With this tremendous growth, it would be a logical assumption that there would also be a natural advancement in human behavior as it relates to the care and respect of human beings, especially children.

Though there has been rapid growth in understanding human behavior, there has been little improvement in human behavior. Sin still exists, and the relationship between godly human virtues and social behavior remains similar to that of the Old Testament era. Unfortunately, resolving this issue is not a matter of advancing human intellect or modern technology. The essence of immoral human behavior is not a matter of the mind but of the soul. Without acknowledging this foundational truth, the quality of life of countless numbers of children within our communities will remain as it has since the days of the Canaanites. Historical evidence bears witness that there has been little improvement in the treatment of children since the Fall of man documented in the book of Genesis.

A Summary of Child Maltreatment

Public opposition to infanticide was rare until modern times. Many Jews considered children who died within thirty days of birth, even by abuse or neglect, to have been a miscarriage. Most ancient societies approved of infanticide, and although Roman law, in response to Christianity, made infanticide a criminal offense in 374 C.E., no documentation of indictments have been discovered. Anglo-Saxons considered infanticide a virtue, saying, "A child cries when he comes into the world, for he anticipates its wretchedness. It is well for him that he should die...he was placed on a slanting roof [and] if he laughed, he was reared, but if he was frightened and cried, he was thrust out to perish.[15]

The overwhelming practice of the mutilation of children's bodies has been found in nearly all cultures in some form. It dates back to the Paleolithic caves where handprints on the walls illustrate that children's fingers were severed from their hands. This was the result of the widespread belief found in many cultures that the Devil (the destructive parental alter) demanded that a child's finger be offered as a sacrifice to satisfy his wrath.[16]

Colin Spencer gives evidence of devastating practices in the Indian, Arab, Chinese, Thailand, and Greek cultures that are inconceivable abuses.[17] The reality of these actions against children must be a stench to God as the rebellion and sin of the people was in Joel's day. The Scripture states, "His stench will come up, and his foul odor will rise, because he has done monstrous things (Joel 2:20).

Pederasty was a common practice among preliterate tribes around the world, from the "customary pederasty" of Australians and the sexual use of berdaches [a person, usually a male, who assumes the gender identity and is given the social status in his community of the opposite sex (a man-woman)]. This occurred in North and Central American tribes where, beginning in infancy, boys were dressed as girls for raping and placed in the role of the "boy-wives" of Africa. Early civilizations practiced boy rape and even had young boys serve as prostitutes in the temples. These practices were included in the following cultures: the ancient Hebrews, Sumerians, Persians, Mesopotamians, Celts, Egyptians, Etruscans, Carthaginians, Chinese, Japanese, Indians, Aztecs, Mayans, etc.[18]

An inscription was excavated at Idalion (an ancient land located at the center of Cyprus in the Mediterranean) in 1974. It was found in the rubble of the citadel wall. An examination of the inscription revealed that it mentions the "holocaust of scion," a reference to a sacrificial burning of a child. The end of the inscription was found to represent the "year 50" (with the 50 represented by the letter nun). This evidence provides the earliest documentation for Phoenician or Western Semitic scribes borrowing the Greek practice of using letters of the alphabet as numbers. Pumayyaton is the only king of Idalion who ruled for fifty years during this period. He reigned from about 362 B.C.E. It is believed that this inscription dates to the year 50 of Pumayyaton, 312 B.C.E., the year of the massive Ptolemaic destruction of the city. This discovery also provides evidence for the practice of child sacrifice among Phoenician populations on the island of Cyprus, and probably also for the existence there of tophets.[19]

There are many who have a passion for uncovering the truth. *National Geographic Magazine* describes an archaeological assistant, Arcadio, who has phenomenal endurance while digging for evidence of child abuse and neglect. He is often found digging long after other team members have stopped to rest. Arcadio is a proud follower of the traditions of his family, whose roots are those of the ancient Incas. Arcadio seems to have developed a sixth sense about archaeological sites. A phenomenal discovery was made at the site of Inca ruins on the summit of Cerro Llullaillaco (pronounced Yu-yai-ya-ko) in the Andes. The discovery was made at approximately 22,110 feet above sea level. Arcadio was the first to make the discovery when he shouted a word that caused all work to stop instantly: "Mummy!" The archaeologists put down their notebooks and hurried over to the place where Arcadio was digging. He and his brother Ignacio had unearthed a section of a stone and gravel platform on the exposed part of the summit where they were digging. "More than five feet below the surface was a bundle wrapped in textiles–the frozen body of an Inca ritual sacrifice, a boy about eight years old...Parts of his arms, hands, and feet were visible and were in excellent condition; his knees were drawn up in a fetal position and bound tightly with a cord. He wore moccasins and white fur anklets, which looked as if they'd been made only yesterday. A broad silver bracelet covered his right wrist."[20]

Other evidence of child abuse in the culture of the Incas has been found in Peru. The Inca Empire had a lifespan of approximately a hundred years and stretched 2,500 miles. As the Incas took control of the area around Cuzco, Peru, they assimilated new people with remarkable effectiveness. They allowed local leaders to keep their positions; however, they would take their sons to Cuzco for training. The families were charged a "labor tax" but were repaid with goods. The Incas believed this honored local gods and religious practices. Through these arrangements they commingled these new people with traditional Inca beliefs and rituals. Unfortunately, child sacrifices were part of this system. The Inca captured children throughout the empire and rewarded their families with goods or positions in society. Sacrifices were seen as unifying events. The children were often taken to Cuzco for celebrations before processions took them on long journeys and up massive mountains to sites where they were sacrificed.[21]

As time progressed, the practice of abandonment may have seemed to be less traumatic to children than physical abuse using various tactics. Autobiographers often mention the deep hurt they experienced as children when they were given away by their parents. Many children in history were, for one excuse or another, either abused or abandoned. One to two-thirds of babies born who were abandoned to foundling homes in the modern era usually died from maltreatment in the institutions that served as orphanages.[22]

The history of voyages from England to Australia provides further historical evidence of a progression of child abuse and neglect. Citing a 17th century law regarding children who were shipped along with some 1500 British adult convicts to Australia in 1788, "The little that has been written on the convict system, however, ignores the fact that some of those transported were children. Fifty of the 1500 First Fleeters were children, some of them convicts."[23] Children are not mentioned in over 200 years of official papers, log books, journals, and inventories. History reduces them to mere footnotes. A major reason is that the children were not seen as being any different than adults and did not receive special care. They were tried and sentenced in the same manner as their adult counterparts. Holden notes, "age by itself gave no right to special treatment and children were tried with the full publicity and formality of the courts."[24]

Historically, abuse and neglect in Africa is similar to that of other nations. Debbie Arroyo reports, "In almost all African countries, there is very little government effort aimed at either regulating or legislating against child abuse. In countries where such legislation exists, very little effort is made at enforcement."[25]

Accounts of child maltreatment throughout history are endless. The aforementioned cases do not begin to adequately describe the inhumane treatment of minors worldwide. The mainstream media fails to mention the staggering statistics provided by the United Nations regarding the women and girls forced into prostitution annually in Thailand, nor have they reported on the multi-billion-dollar business of the global trafficking of Haitian Restavecs (child slaves).

In many contexts there has always been a lack of care, compassion, and protection for children while predators and neglectors alike have viewed them as a means to a self-centered, self-serving end. Children have been little more than objects of sexual pleasure, pawns of domestic servitude, anger-management outlets, and in many cases afterthoughts in the lives of parents too busy to adequately care for their children.

Within the last two hundred years, efforts have been made to bring an end to these acts in the United States. Mary Ellen was a little child living in a New York neighborhood in 1873–1874. A church worker who lived near Mary Ellen observed her deplorable physical condition. The neighbor saw that Mary Ellen was undernourished and poorly dressed. She estimated that the child was approximately five years of age only to discover that in actuality she was nine years old. In a desperate attempt to help this child, the church worker sought help from the *New York Society for the Prevention of Cruelty to Animals*. Agency staff removed Mary Ellen from her home. She had been physically neglected and physically abused by her adoptive parents. The actual charge brought against the adoptive parents was that of cruelty to an animal of the human species.

As a result of the incident involving Mary Ellen, the *New York Society for the Prevention of Cruelty to Children* was established in 1875. Mary Ellen's case also stirred the founding of the first *Society for the Prevention of Cruelty to Children in London* (1884), with the ensuing development of the *Scottish National Society for the Prevention of Cruelty to Children* (1889).

How ironic it is that there was public sympathy for the inhumane treatment of animals, as evidenced by the existence of the *New York Society for the Prevention of Cruelty to Animals*, yet there were no existing entities of compassion available for a child like Mary Ellen. There were agencies established whose efforts were aimed toward protecting orphans. However, there were legal constraints prohibiting intervention by law enforcement to protect the welfare of children who were in the custody of their parents. Children were considered as the property of their parents. This thinking restricted law enforcement's ability to investigate alleged cases of child maltreatment.

A Theology of Sin

This brief overview of child maltreatment illustrates a pervasive problem that has been part of humanity for centuries. Abuse and neglect are not confined to a particular culture, era, race, or socioeconomic class, but are issues of sin that has affected every generation since the corporate fall of humanity in the Garden of Eden. Historical, archaeological, and biblical evidence has demonstrated that this sin has plagued our societies without much relief. Non-believers have attempted to address this immoral behavior without addressing its root cause–sin. Christians have embraced an attitude of indifference as they delegate the oversight of a biblical problem (Satan and sin) to governmental agencies without offering any assistance. This hands-off approach is unfortunate. Kerry Skinner stated that, "If sin is the problem, there is no human remedy."[26] Good solutions to sin problems must be grounded in biblical principles found in the Word of God.

The main perpetrator, Satan, uses one of humanity's biggest weaknesses, pride, to thwart efforts to resolve this sin. Humans (especially in western culture) have the innate need to rationalize all aspects of life through their intellect. This has resulted in a failed protective system for children and the destruction of countless families. Without relying on the sovereign Word of God, man has attempted to establish his own system to address child maltreatment. The world's thinking does not consider the influence of the adversary nor the issue of sin when constructing strategic methods to effectively deal with child maltreatment.

The Nature of Sin

By definition, sin is a breach of the will of the LORD as a result of man's rebellious heart and self-centered motives and intentions. Bruce Marino writes,

> perhaps the best definition of sin is found in 1 John 3:4–"Sin is lawlessness." Whatever else sin is, at its heart, it is a breach of God's law. And since "all wrongdoing is sin" (1 John 5:17) all wrongdoing breaks God's law. So David confesses, "Against you, you only, have I sinned" (Ps. 51:4; Luke 15:18, 21). Furthermore, transgression forces separation from the God of Life and Holiness, which necessarily results in the corruption (including death) of finite, dependent human nature. Therefore, this definition of sin is biblical, precise, and embraces every type of sin; it accounts for sin's effects on nature and is referenced to God, not humanity. That is, we see its true nature by observing its contrast to God, not by comparing its effects among human beings.[27]

Sin therefore encompasses all evil, including self-centeredness, perversion, guilt, hate, rage, murder, sensuality, rebellion, debauchery, and unbelief. Its characteristics are those of its originator, Satan. "Sin, the product of the 'father of lies' (John 8:44), is the antithesis of God's truth (Ps. 31:5; John 14:6; 1 John 5:20)...From the first it has deceived in what it promised...It can give dramatic, but only temporary pleasure."[28]

In essence, sin is all that is contrary to the word and nature of God. The LORD's Word represents His true nature. His Word gives humanity the blueprint for wholesome, life-honoring interaction while here on earth. As the main perpetrator was discussed earlier it was mentioned that Satan wants to "steal, kill, and destroy" (John 10:10). That is not the end of the verse, nor is it the end of the story. Jesus then declares, "I came that they may have life, and have it abundantly." Jesus Christ has conquered Satan and all evil that exists. He has also provided for every need of mankind by the work that was accomplished in his death, resurrection, and ascension. He must be included in the battle against the adversary if man is to successfully defeat the sin of child maltreatment.

Chapter 1 has laid the foundation of the origin and progression of child maltreatment. Chapter 2 examines four major areas in which this sin has been manifested. Social workers have identified these areas of child maltreatment and are working locally, nationally, and internationally to combat the perpetrators of abuse and neglect. The issue of sin, which is at the heart of the problem, is included in the discussion of these areas.

---

[1] *Child Maltreatment 2007*, (Washington, D.C.: U.S. Government Printing Office, United States Department of Health and Human Services, Administration on Children, Youth and Families, 2002), Table 3-10.

[2] Neil Postman, *Amusing Ourselves to Death: Public Discourse in the Age of Show Business*, (New York, NY, Penguin Books, 1984), 104-105.

[3] Bob DeWaay, *Biblical Counseling, Part 2: Getting to the Root of the Problem*, (Critical Issues Commentary), [http://cicministry.org/commentary/issue9.htm], November 14, 2006.

[4] Henry Brandt and Kerry Skinner, *The Heart of the Problem* (Nashville, Tennessee, Broadman & Holman, 1997), 73.

[5] Jonathan Tubb, *Canaanites: Peoples of the Past* (Norman, OK, University of Oklahoma, 1998), 75.

[6] John Day, *Molech: A God of Human Sacrifice in the Old Testament* (Cambridge: Cambridge University Press, 1989), 86-91.

[7] Shelby Brown, *Late Carthaginian Child Sacrifice and Sacrificial Monuments In Their Mediterranean Context* (Sheffield: JSOT Press, 1991), 26–29.

[8] Bob Boyd, *Baal Worship in Old Testament Days*, (Scranton, PA., Vernon Martin & Associates, 1966), 15.

[9] Ibid., 15.

[10] Lawrence E. Stager and Samuel R. Wolff, *Child Sacrifice at Carthage: Religious Rite or Population Control?* (Biblical Archeological Review, January, 1984) 31–46.

[11] Joseph P. Free, *Archaeology and Bible History*, (Grand Rapids, MI, Zondervan, 1992), 34-54.

[12] Nigel Davies, *Human Sacrifices: In History and Today*, (New York, Morrow, 1981), 51.

[13] Ibid., 64–65.

[14] Bob Boyd, *Baal Worship*, 16.

[15] Lloyd deMause, *Emotional Life of Nations* (New York & London, Karnac, 2002), 305–306.

[16] Ibid., 307.

[17] Ibid., 352–353, 371 (Colin Spencer states that throughout Indian history, "Mothers stimulated the penises of their infants and gave a 'deep massage' to their daughters as a form of affectionate consolation." It has been discovered that Arab mothers "rub the penis long and energetically to increase its size," "In China, Manchu mothers tickle the genitals of their little daughters and suck the penis of a small son," "In Thailand, mothers habitually stroke their son's genitals." In Greek pederasty, the cultural practice of domination as opposed to tender love was the focus of all sexuality until modern times. The sexual preference of men was to rape boys, as it was considered more "according to nature" than heterosexuality, "an ordinance enacted by divine laws."

[18] Ibid.

[19] F. M. Cross, *A Phoenician Inscription from Idalion: Some Old and New Testament Texts Relating to Child Sacrifice* (Scripture and Other Artifacts. Louisville: Westminster John Knox, 1994), 93-107.

[20] Johan Reinhard, "At 22,000 Feet Children of Inca Sacrifice Found Frozen In Time", (*National Geographic*, 196, no. 5, November 1999), 40.

[21] Ibid., 42.

[22] Lloyd deMause, *The Evolution of Childrearing*, (Journal of Psychohistory, 28, no. 4, Spring 2001, 415.

[23] Robert Holden, *Orphans of History–The Forgotten Children of the First Fleet* (The Text Publishing Company, 1999), [http://www.wsws.org/articles/2001/feb2001/orph-f20_prn.shtml.].

[24] Ibid.

[25] Ariyo, Debbie, *The Future Lost: The Economic and Social Consequences of Child Abuse in Africa*, [http://africaeconomicanalysis.rg/articles/gen/childabusehtm.html].

[26] Kerry L. Skinner, *The Joy of Repentance* (Mobile, AL, KLS LifeChange Ministries, 2006), 37.

[27] Bruce R. Marino, *Systematic Theology* (Springfield, MO, Logion Press, 2003), 273.

[28] Ibid., 276.

Chapter Two
An Unbelievable Reality

"My people are destroyed for lack of knowledge. Because you
have rejected knowledge, I also reject you from being My priest."

Hosea 4:6

Contemporary social problems challenge the well-being of
today's family. What keeps people from improving on these poor
living conditions? We have incredible knowledge, history, and
experience on our side to coach us in making intelligent decisions
for improved living. This knowledge could lead us to strengthen
social behavior and produce crime free living. Seldom, however, do
we learn our lesson from observing history. As a result, our problems do not stem from a lack of information but from a rejection or
total disregard of readily accessible information.

During Hosea's era the Lord's anger burned against the priests
as they rejected the revelation of God's Word. Lloyd Ogilvie writes,
"God's diagnosis of Israel's spiritual illness was because of the lack
of clear teaching of the Torah, His people were being destroyed
because of a lack of knowledge of Him."[1] The priests neglected
their role as spiritual leaders of Israel and developed a distorted
identity because of their disobedience and lack of faith.

The emphasis of Hosea 4:6 relates to the children of Israel's
diminished knowledge and understanding of the nature, laws, and

will of God. James Mays writes, "knowledge is learning and obey-
ing the will of the covenant of God in devotion and faithfulness; it
is response to the unity of Yahweh's saving act and binding require-
ment such as is expressed in 'I am Yahweh your God who brought
you up out of the land of Egypt, out of the house of slavery. You
shall have no other gods before me' (Exodus 20:2–3)."[2]
Undoubtedly the priests were negligent in conveying these truths to
God's people. As a result, their participation in idolatrous worship
led to inhumane sacrifices.

Throughout history many social injustices could possibly have
been avoided had the truth of God's Word been practically applied
in the lives of those that were privileged to hear the gospel. Relative
to those social injustices Ogilvie writes, "Think back over the past
three decades of the battles for social justice. It is no pleasure to
remember that causes such as equal rights and racial integration had
to climb over the stiff backs of good church people with an inadequate knowledge of God. Even more appalling were some clergy
who refused to stand up and be counted by preaching the truth."[3]
The truth of God's Word provides insight to every generation
whether it be to those of Hosea's time, those who stood for truth
during the civil rights era, or to those who stand shoulder to shoulder in the war against child maltreatment.

More knowledge and information is available and accessible
today than at any other time in human history. Those that have lived
in the western world have had a monopoly on information and technology. That has shifted in the past 15 years, according to journalist
Thomas Friedman. Friedman writes, "But Globalization 3.0 differs
from the previous eras not only in how it is shrinking and flattening
the world and in how it is empowering individuals…Globalization
3.0 makes it possible for so many more people to plug in and play,
and you are going to see every color of the human rainbow take

part."[4] Our world is indeed "flattening" through accessible information and technology available on the internet. There is a dire need for the Christian community to develop an aggressive posture and strategically involve themselves in the battle against child maltreatment by taking advantage of available information in our "flattening" world. Knowledge of the comprehensive nature of child maltreatment can provide the wisdom to combat this social injustice that has plagued the world for centuries. Following is a working definition of child maltreatment and the four divisions of child maltreatment.

Child Maltreatment

Child

The terms of child abuse and neglect refers specifically to parents and other caregivers. A child under this definition generally means a person who is under the age of 18 or who is not an emancipated minor. In cases of child sexual abuse, a child is one who has not attained the age of 18 or the age specified by the child protection law of the state in which the child resides, whichever is younger.[5]

Child Abuse and Neglect

Any recent act or failure to act on the part of a parent or caretaker that results in death, serious physical or emotional harm, sexual abuse, or exploitation, or that presents an imminent risk of serious harm, is considered child maltreatment.[6]

These definitions are adopted from the *Federal Child Abuse Prevention and Treatment Act* (CAPTA). In addition to these definitions, each state is given the liberty to develop its own definitions based upon state legislation and corresponding criminal and civil codes. It is nationally recognized that "there is great variation from

State to State regarding the details and specificity of child abuse definitions, but it is still possible to identify commonalities among each different type of child maltreatment."[7] Child abuse and neglect statutes for each state are located on the *Child Welfare Information Gateway* website.[8]

The Four Maltreatments

Child abuse and neglect is generally characterized by four maltreatments. Slight variations in the definitions of child maltreatment are found in both interstate and intrastate legislation. However, most incidents of abuse and neglect are defined by one of the following maltreatments: *neglect, physical abuse, sexual abuse*, or *mental injury*. As previously stated, each state is given the liberty to establish legislation within the parameters of the *Child Abuse Prevention and Treatment Act*. In developing strategic measures to effectively combat child maltreatment, it is imperative that citizens have a clear knowledge of the governing laws and definitions of the state (or country if living outside of the United States) in which they reside.

Along with the four maltreatments, there are two other related terms that will assist in establishing a better understanding of child maltreatment. These terms are *indicators* and *dynamics*. Physical indicators are those manifestations that a person can see, hear, smell, or touch. Dynamics are the observed behavioral tendencies of those that have been abused or neglected, as well as those of their family members and other caregivers. These behavioral dynamics are observed through daily interaction. The functioning of the family unit and caregivers may provide insight as to whether or not abuse and neglect may be occurring.

Many indicators and dynamics may overlap. Therefore, it is highly probable that some of them will be found in more than one of the four categories. Caution must be taken whenever indicators or dynamics are observed within families or individuals. The presence of specific indicators or dynamics does not necessarily mean that abuse and neglect are occurring. These are viewed by social workers as red flags that *may* serve as a catalyst for further investigation by a trained professional. Some of the dynamics and indicators are quite common behaviors that occur at certain ages within the life of a child, and are not the result of abuse or neglect.

Neglect

The most common form of child maltreatment is *neglect*. The following definitions are provided by federal legislation:

Child Neglect–a failure to provide for a child's basic needs. Neglect can be physical, educational, or emotional.

Physical Neglect includes a refusal of health care, a delay in health care, abandonment, expulsion from home without arranging adequate care, inadequate supervision, inadequate personal care (i.e., hygiene, nutrition, clothing, conspicuous inattention to avoid hazards, reckless disregard of a child's safety and welfare, leaving a child in a car unattended, and driving DUI with a child in the car).

Educational Neglect includes the allowance of permitted chronic truancy of a child of mandatory school age in school, and failure to attend to a special educational need.

Emotional Neglect includes such actions as marked inattention to the child's needs for affection; refusal of or failure to provide needed psychological care; spouse abuse in the child's presence; and permission of drug or alcohol use by the child, other permitted maladaptive behavior (e.g., chronic delinquency, severe assault), refusal or a delay of psychological care.

Please Note: The assessment of child neglect requires the careful consideration of cultural values and standards of care as well as recognition that the failure to provide the necessities of life may be related to poverty (which is not neglect, but consequently needs to be addressed).[9]

According to data collected by the *U.S. Department of Health and Human Services*, "more than half of the reported victims (62.8 percent) suffered neglect (including medical neglect)."[10] The report also reveals that during the same period (the year 2000) when the statistics were gathered "there were an estimated 879,000 victims of maltreatment nationwide"[11] that were actually reported. Even though the actual number of children that were maltreated during this period is unknown because of a lack of reporting, among other factors, the data reflects an astonishing number of children that were neglected: 552,012. Compared to the other maltreatments (i.e., physical abuse, sexual abuse, mental injury) neglect may not appear to be particularly devastating, but an examination of a case study that involves child neglect reveals otherwise. Maria Piers shares a case study that illustrates this:

> On November 12, 1934, a male child was born in Cincinnati, Ohio. It is reported that this child was born as the result of rape. His mother, sixteen-year-old Kathleen Maddox, was not ready for motherhood. The child's birth certificate is evidence of this as it reads: "No Name Maddox." With little support from the biological father, No Name Maddox bounded around between the home of a grandparent and a maternal aunt as his mother would disappear for days and weeks at a time, leaving the baby 'for an hour.' His mother was arrested in 1939 for armed robbery and was sentenced to the West Virginia state penitentiary. The young "Maddox" child was sent to live with an aunt and uncle in West Virginia who reportedly had a difficult marriage. At the end of her sentence, when young Maddox was eight, Ms. Maddox regained custody of her son and began living with "a long line of uncles" who, along with Ms. Maddox, drank heavily. Home was considered a variety of run-down hotel rooms in which young Maddox was often forced to stay alone all day. His mother made arrangements for him to stay with foster parents but unfortunately this only lasted for approximately one year. According to a report, young Maddox received very little atten-

tion from his mother or the many men that she lived with. He
ended up in many state institutions himself, one of which was
the *Gibault Home for Boys* in Terre Haute, Indiana, where the
children were disciplined with the rod and whip. He eventually
ran away and tried to reunite with his mother. Unfortunately,
she made it clear that she did not want him. Young Maddox
began a life of crime ranging from burglary to murder.[12]

In an effort to understand the potential seriousness of child neglect the identity of young Maddox needs to be revealed. Maddox
later gained national attention in the early 1970's as one of the most
feared serial killers in the United States. He is none other than
Charles Manson. Manson, with the assistance of several members
of his cult, committed several homicides, including the murder of a
mother and her unborn child. He is currently serving a life sentence
for his role in the gruesome murders of several individuals and was
denied parole for the ninth time in 1997.[13] Years after his imprisonment the crimes that he masterminded remain etched in the minds
of people all over the world.

The case study of Manson is the exception and not the rule in
cases of child neglect. Not every person who has been neglected
during childhood develops homicidal tendencies. However, the following statement made by Piers is worth noting:

> One might object, rightfully, that a highly publicized case such
> as Charles Manson's does not prove anything. And of course it
> does not, for, as we know, not every brutalized and grossly neg-
> lected child grows up to be a Charles Manson. On the other
> hand, virtually every Charles Manson was once a neglected and
> abused child.[14]

The aforementioned statistics reveal that over 500,000 children
were neglected during the year 2000. It may never be known how
many of them will be adversely affected by the lack of attention and
how many may become grossly affected by maltreatment as did

Manson. However, preventive measures need to be taken to help ensure that the possibility of the development of dysfunctional behavior is minimized.

The chart on the next page provides the physical indicators and behavioral dynamics that professionals have identified as being associated with child neglect. God's people need to also become informed so that they can ask for help if they observe these conditions.

Although Figure 2-1 is not an exhaustive list of the indicators and dynamics of child neglect, it offers insight and understanding into what a child may be experiencing. Observing a child's behavior may reveal the type of interaction, or lack thereof, between family members resulting in a possible incident of neglect. From what has been noted, it would be wrong to assume that child neglect is less damaging to the well-being of a child than physical, sexual, and emotional abuse. Child neglect is the most prevalent of the four maltreatments and deserves as much diligence and attention as the others.

The Lord provides insight to the care of children in Proverbs 22:6: "Train up a child in the way he should go: and when he is old he will not depart from it." The training of children in this passage refers to the process of shaping and molding a child's life from infancy through the formative years and into adulthood. The *New King James Study Bible* provides an explanation of this passage as it relates to neglecting children. "The biblical pattern of effective parental training emphasizes the balance of instruction and discipline. The ideal parent is to be neither overly authoritarian nor overly permissive. Rather, he must balance love and discipline so as not to 'provoke' his child to rebellion."[15]

Figure 2-1
Child Neglect Indicators & Dynamics

Source: South Carolina Department of Social Services[16]

Child Neglect	Physical <u>Indicators</u>: Child	Behavioral <u>Dynamics</u>: Child
	Consistent hunger, malnourished, anemic or emaciated	Begging or stealing food for necessity
	Consistent lack of supervision, especially in dangerous activities for long periods	Extended stays at school (frequent early arrival & late departure)
	Abandonment	Rare attendance at school
	Intellectually dull parent, IQ below 70	Constant fatigue, listlessness or falling asleep in class
	Inadequate or inappropriate dress for weather	Delayed speech
	Dressed in clothes that are dirty, that have a bad odor, or are constantly in need of repair	Inappropriate seeking of affection
	Child is physically dirty and skin has a bad odor	Doesn't change expression
	Chronic or acute medical problems that go unattended	Assuming adult responsibilities and concerns
	Has not received immunizations or other preventive health care	Alcohol and drug use
	Suffers from chronic, low-level illness	Delinquency (i.e., thefts)
	Has persistent hygiene related health problems, scabies, lice, diaper rash, ringworm, etc.	Involved in age inappropriate sexual behavior
	Garbage and excrement in living areas	School failure and academic under-achievement
	Has not received necessary prosthetics such as glasses, hearing aides, braces.	Showing signs of sexual victimization.
	Exposed electrical wiring	States that there is no caretaker and that none is needed
	Broken glass and other environmental hazards in living area	Demonstrates bizarre eating or other food-related habits
	Home infested with rodents or insects	Has history of poor academic progress and scholastic adjustment
	Unclean source of drinking water	Demonstrates suspicion, pessimism, distrust, and depression
	Drugs or poisons kept within reach of children	Often appears preoccupied of even day-dreaming
	Home is unheated during cold or freezing weather	

Physical Abuse

Often physical injuries to children are the result of poor impulse control by their caregivers. There are literally hundreds of child homicides each year in the United States that can be attributed to poor impulsive decisions made by those whose duty it is to provide a safe, nurturing environment for them. According to data collected by the *Department of Health and Human Services*, "a nationally estimated 1,200 children died [in the year 2000] of abuse or neglect–a rate of 1.71 children per 100,000 children in the population."[17] This figure does not take into account the number of child deaths that are unreported in the United States or the death of children worldwide who reside in countries where statistics related to abuse and neglect are not gathered.

Physical abuse is any deliberate infliction of physical injury to a child or the allowing of physical injury to children. According to federal legislation, physical abuse is defined as follows:

> Abuse that is characterized by the infliction of physical injury as a result of punching, beating, kicking, biting, burning, shaking, throwing, stabbing, choking, hitting with a hand, stick, strap, or other object. The parent or caretaker may not have intended to hurt the child; rather, the injury may have resulted from over-discipline or physical punishment.

> Although an injury resulting from physical abuse is not accidental, the parent or caregiver may not have intended to hurt the child. The injury may have resulted from severe discipline, including injurious spanking, or physical punishment that is inappropriate to the child's age or condition. The injury may be the result of a single episode or of repeated episodes and can range in severity from minor marks and bruising to death.[18]

Some practices related to varying cultures may result in physically harming a child, such as coining (forcefully rubbing a coin on

48

the flesh to treat an illness). Cultural practices are taken into account when investigating child maltreatment; however, the safety of children cannot be jeopardized and must have higher priority than cultural preferences.

It is reported that "166,232 children (or 19.3% of all founded cases reported) were physically abused in the year 2000."[19] The effects of physical abuse can be devastating to a child physically, mentally, and emotionally. To assist in understanding the effects of physical abuse the following case study provides evidence relative of the consequences of this maltreatment.

On March 13, 1933, a male child known as "Junior Parrott" (Parrott being his mother's maiden name) was born in rural Florence, South Carolina. He was later given the name "Pee Wee" because of his small stature. Little Junior Parrott lived with his mother but never knew his father, as he was born an illegitimate child. As his mother allowed a series of "step-daddies" access to Junior, he began being beaten and neglected by both mom and her partners. In 1943 Junior's mother married one of the men and subsequently bore four other children for her husband. Junior Parrott reported that his "step-daddy" beat him and the other children "just for practice", as violence was a part of everyday life in the household. Even though this was the case, Junior stated, "I certainly weren't in no way what you could ever call abused." A maladjusted Junior Parrott developed poor relational skills and suffered from fits of unexplainable rage. The Crime Library reports that by age 10 he was suffering from a lifelong "bothersomeness," which he described as feeling like "a ball of molten lead rolling around in my guts and up my spine into my head." Ultimately, increasingly violent behavior ensued which lead the young man into a life of criminal activity at an early age (that included rape, burglary, and assault with a deadly weapon with intent to kill). Junior was sentenced to the state reformatory where he received what he called his "real education." While in reformatory he was repeatedly beaten by guards for a variety of rule infractions and gang raped by fellow juveniles. Junior Parrott's life evolved around numerous stints in correctional institutions where he experienced similar treatment. He committed heinous crimes while he was incarcerated and dozens more after his release.[20]

Many in the southeastern region of the United States know Junior Parrott by his given name, Donald Henry "Pee Wee" Gaskins. Pee Wee, like Charles Manson, became a ruthless serial killer infamous for the brutal methods used to torture his victims before taking their lives. Reports reveal that Gaskins raped, sodomized, tortured, mutilated, cooked, and cannibalized the severed genitals of some of his victims. Gaskins conscience appeared unfazed by the horrific nature of the crimes he committed. Before his execution he claimed to have killed between eighty and ninety people.

As previously stated, there were 166,232 reported cases of physical abuse in the United States in the year 2000. The adversary of our souls, Satan, would like nothing more than to influence many of those that were physically abused to the degree that he influenced "Pee Wee" Gaskins. The following charts offer an in-depth view of the behavioral indicators of parents and families along with physical indicators and behavioral dynamics of children that have been physically abused.

Just as the indicators and dynamics related to physical neglect should be viewed as red flags that may indeed warrant further investigation by social work and law enforcement professionals, so should the indicators and dynamics of physical abuse be viewed.

Figure 2-2
Behavioral Indicators: Parents and Families
(Related to Physical Abuse)
Source: South Carolina Department of Social Services[21]

Physical Abuse	Behavioral Indicators: Parents	Behavioral Indicators: Familial
	Chronic use of poor judgment in decision-making	History of substance abuse
	Pervasiveness of neglectful behavior, not of the child but also of herself/himself	Often began having children at a very young age (i.e., 16 yrs. old or younger)
	Repetition of the same mistakes; inability to learn from experience	Home life is chaotic and disorganized
	Low level of energy; sometimes interspersed with periods of frenzied activity	History of unemployment or underemployment
	Extreme sensitivity to criticism	Lack of adequate education and/or job training
	Passive-aggressive and manipulative interactions with child protective services and other figures of authority	Have no areas of their life where they have experienced success
	Verbally inaccessible	Have little motivation or skills to effect change.
	Immature and egocentric	No close or satisfying personal relationships
	Leaves older children to fend for themselves for long periods of time	Family of origin was abusive and/or neglectful
	Chronically misses appointments regarding his/her child's care	Little parental planning or sharing
	Inability to delay gratification	Limited knowledge of child development
	Emotional numbness	Physically, socially, and/or psychologically isolated
	Inability to tolerate stress or frustration	Neglect is pervasive within a family (most likely will be focused on just one child)
	Turns to her children to meet his/her needs and assume a care-taking role	
	Parent fails to get prescribed medication, although financially able to do so (and they are aware of how to obtain help)	
	Parent fails to administer medication or other treatment when they have the needed supplies	
	Exaggerated dependent behavior	
	Lacks the capacity to empathize with his/her children	
	Has difficulty in building trust in relationships	
	Preoccupied with own frustrations	
	Depressed and apathetic	
	Distrust others & feels helpless to change	

Figure 2-3
Physical Abuse Indicators and Dynamics: Child
Source: South Carolina Department of Social Services[22]

Physical Abuse	Physical Indicators: <u>Child</u>	Behavioral (Dynamics): <u>Child</u>
	Unexplained Bruises & Welts •on face, lips, mouth •torso, back, buttocks, thighs •in various stages of healing •clustered, forming rectangular patterns (or reflecting shape of article used to inflict pain–electric cord, belt buckle, etc. •on several different surface areas •regularly appear after absence, weekend, or vacation	*Behavioral Extremes* •aggressiveness or withdrawal •frightened of parents •afraid to go home •reports of injury by parents •vacant or frozen stare •lies very still while surveying surrounding (infants) •responds to questions in monosyllable •inappropriate or precocious maturity •manipulative behavior to get attention •capable of only superficial relationships •indiscriminately seeks affection •poor self-concept
	Unexplained Burns •cigar burns, cigarette burns (especially on soles of feet, palms of hand, back, or buttocks) •immersion burns (sock-like, glove-like, doughnut shaped on buttocks or genitalia) •patterns (like electric burner, iron, space heater etc.) •rope burns on arms, legs, neck or torso •infected burns (indicating delay in seeking treatment)	*Other Behavioral Dynamics:* *(CHILD)* •Feels deserving of punishment •Wary of adult contact •Apprehensive when other children cry
	Unexplained Lacerations or Abrasions •to mouth, lips, gums or eyes •to external genitalia •in various stages of healing •bald patches on the scalp	

Sexual Abuse

Arguably the most publicized form of child maltreatment is sexual abuse. Reports of child rape, sodomy, pornography, and prostitution are aired weekly as national and international awareness and advocacy have gained momentum. Those that have been indicted on charges of pedophilia span the demographic spectrum. Religious leaders, community leaders, politicians, and average citizens have fallen to the temptation of child exploitation. In some countries child prostitution and the trafficking of children have become major illegal industries with annual profits soaring into billions.

Recent reports have revealed prevalent, yet rarely publicized, incidents of sexual abuse by female perpetrators. The source of each of the four maltreatments, Satan, has deceived many in society by having the most attention focused on male perpetrators. Female pedophilia is just as damaging as sexual crimes committed by males; however, rarely do female perpetrators receive the same amount of attention. More discussion of perpetrators and pedophiles follow later.

Federal legislation provides the following definition for the sexual maltreatment of children:

Sexual Abuse–The employment, use, persuasion, inducement, enticement, or coercion of any child to engage in, or assist any other person to engage in, any sexually explicit conduct or simulation of such conduct for the purpose of producing visual depiction of such conduct;

The rape, and in cases of caretaker or inter-familial relationships, statutory rape, molestation, prostitution, or other form of sexual exploitation of children, or incest with children.[23]

Child sexual abuse generally refers to sexual acts, sexually motivated behaviors involving children, or sexual exploitation of children. Child sexual abuse includes a wide range of behaviors, such as:

- Oral, anal, or genital penetration;
- Anal or genital digital penetration;
- Genital contact with no intrusion;
- Fondling of a child's breasts or buttocks;
- Indecent exposure;
- Inadequate or inappropriate supervision of a child's voluntary sexual activities
- Use of a child in prostitution, pornography, Internet crimes, or other sexually exploitive activitie[24]

Indicated cases (those cases found to have enough substantiated evidence that result in a guilty verdict) of sexual abuse range in the tens of thousands each year. In the year 2000, 10.1%, or 87,480 children were reportedly sexually abused in the United States.[25] However staggering 87,000 indicated annual reports may appear, professionals concur that these numbers are conservative and represent only a portion of the sexual victimization of children in the United States. There is no way to accurately determine what sexual maltreatments are occurring on a global scale. Christian missionaries who serve in countries outside of America regularly share reports of legalized prostitution of young girls and boys who are sold by their parents to pay off debts or simply for monetary gain.[26] Many of these children are sold on the black market as sex slaves before they reach their teenage years. The following chart provides the physical indicators and behavioral dynamics associated with sexual abuse.

As with the other maltreatments, the list of indicators and dynamics listed for sexual abuse is not exhaustive; however, it illustrates numerous behavioral traits exhibited by children who have been sexually maltreated. As with the other maltreatments, if a child displays any of the behaviors listed in isolation or a combination of behavioral dynamics, it does not necessarily mean that the child has been sexually abused. These behaviors would serve as red flags that warrant further investigation by a professional. Any attempt by someone who has not been trained to investigate alleged maltreatment could contaminate a case and possibly severely damage a child and the family.

Figure 2-4
Sexual Abuse Indicators and Dynamics: Child
Source: South Carolina Department of Social Services[27]

Sexual Abuse	Physical Indicators: <u>Child</u>	Behavioral Dynamics: <u>Child</u>
	Difficulty in walking or sitting	Unwilling to change for gym or participate in physical education class
	Stained, torn, or bloody underclothing	Poor peer relationships
	Pain, swelling, or itching in the genital area	Unusual, bizarre, or sophisticated sexual behavior or knowledge
	Bruises, bleeding or lacerations in external genitalia, vaginal, or anal areas	Infantile behavior, fantasizing, or withdrawal from others
	Vaginal or penile discharge	Delinquent or runaway
	Venereal disease, especially in pre-teenage years	Reports of sexual assault by caretaker
	Poor sphincter tone *Sphincter according to Websters definition–a ringlike muscle that closes a bodily passage or orifice–example being the anus)*	Change in academic performance in school (both positively or negatively)
	Pregnancy	

Figure 2-5
Other Behavioral Dynamics Related to Child Sexual Abuse
Source: South Carolina Department of Social Services[28]

Other Behavioral Dynamics

- Unexplained regression in a child's developmental milestones; thumb sucking, soiling, baby talk, excessive clinging behavior;
- Statements that he/she has been sexually abused or hints of such activity or victimization;
- Unusually seductive behavior with peers or adults;
- Expressions through a child's artwork, journaling, poetry, or stories;
- Psychosomatic preoccupation and/or complaints;
- Periods of unexplained crying, anxiety, or fear;
- Enuresis (urinating involuntarily on oneself) or Encopresis (involuntary defecation);
- Age inappropriate sexual preoccupation (i.e., masturbation, genital play with peers and younger children, promiscuity);
- Self Mutilation;
- Physical complaints such as a pain in the throat or abdominal area (which may indicate actual physical damage done to these areas);
- Anger or dislike or fear of known adults;
- Blaming or disliking oneself;
- Poor socialization skills with peers;
- Dating significantly older men;
- Prostitution;
- Substance abuse.

Promiscuity, prostitution, alcoholism, substance abuse, and scores of other dysfunctional behaviors have been widely documented by social workers as being associated with this maltreatment. With the frequent reports of sexual abuse publicized weekly, it is unnecessary to provide a case study regarding this maltreatment. A proper perspective regarding this maltreatment can be gained by reviewing the behavioral dynamics in Figure 2-4 and Figure 2-5. Following is a discussion of the last of the four divisions of child maltreatment, emotional abuse.

Emotional Abuse

With sexual abuse being arguably the most publicized form of child maltreatment, the least publicized and one of the most difficult to prove is emotional abuse. This maltreatment has been categorized in various ways, such as mental injury, psychological maltreatment, verbal abuse, and emotional abuse. However defined, emotional abuse can result in the same level of trauma as the three previously mentioned maltreatments.

Out of the 862,455 identified cases of child maltreatment in the year 2000, 66,293 (or 7.7%) of them were attributed to psychological maltreatment.[29] In order to prove that emotional abuse (or psychological maltreatment) has occurred, social workers have to provide detailed documentation and need supporting evidence from a mental health or medical professional. According to the report provided by the *Department of Health and Human Services*,

> Psychological maltreatment is the most difficult form of child maltreatment to identify. In part, the difficulty in detection occurs because the effects of psychological maltreatment, such as lags in development, learning problems, and speech disorders, are often evident in both children who have experienced and those who have not experienced maltreatment. Additionally, the effects of psychological maltreatment may only become evident in later developmental stages of the child's life.[30]

The difficulty in determining cases of emotional abuse further emphasizes the need for intervention by God's people. God has provided everyone access to knowledge that can assist in preventing and identifying child maltreatment. The following definition provides insight into the most difficult maltreatment to detect.

Emotional **Abuse**–Psychological maltreatment, also known as emotional abuse and neglect–refers to "a repeated pattern of caregiver behavior or extreme incident(s) that convey to children that they are worthless, flawed, unloved, unwanted, endangered, or only of value in meeting another's needs. Summarizing research and expert opinion, Stuart N. Hart, Ph.D., and Marla R. Brassard, Ph.D., present six categories of psychological maltreatment:

- Spurning (e.g., belittling, hostile rejecting, ridiculing);
- Terrorizing (e.g., threatening violence against a child, placing a child in [a] recognizably dangerous situation);
- Isolating (e.g., confining the child, placing unreasonable limitations on the child's freedom of movement, restricting the child from social interactions);
- Exploiting or corrupting (e.g., modeling antisocial behavior such as criminal activities, encouraging prostitution, permitting substance abuse);
- Denying emotional responsiveness (e.g., ignoring the child's attempts to interact, failing to express affection);
- Mental health, medical, and educational neglect (e.g., refusing to allow or failing to provide treatment for serious mental health or medical problems, ignoring the need for services for serious educational needs.)[31]

Two passages of Scripture give further instruction to parents and caregivers concerning the emotional health of children. In Ephesians 6:4 the apostle Paul exhorts the men of Ephesus with the following statement: "Fathers, do not provoke your children to anger, but bring them up in the discipline and instruction of the Lord." Paul repeats this biblical principle in his letter to the church in Colossae. Each book was likely penned by Paul in his first imprisonment in Rome. He undoubtedly felt the need to express his concerns about the treatment of children in both communities. Colossians 3:21 states "Fathers, do not exasperate your children, that they may not lose heart." The passage implies that fathers can provoke their children by treating them unjustly, losing their temper with them, imposing undue severity and cruelty upon them, show-ing favoritism, ridiculing them, being sarcastic or misusing and/or abusing parental authority. Each of these scriptural injunctions is directly related to forbidding the emotional abuse of a child. The Word of God is clear regarding the psychological treatment of chil-dren. Constant berating can leave children scarred for life and sub-sequently affect the way in which they perceive themselves. This will directly affect the paths that they may choose in life, and the way in which they relate to others.

An example of the effects of emotional abuse can be found in the case study of Henry Lee Lucas. Lucas came from an excessive-ly dysfunctional home. His mother, Viola, was the major perpetra-tor. Reports reveal that "when he was old enough to attend school, his mother taunted him by curling his hair and sending him to school in a dress…This insensitive act by his mother caused him to be "teased and ridiculed by classmates."[32] His teacher, having sym-pathy for him, cut the curls off of his head and provided him with appropriate clothing, which infuriated his mother so much that she verbally confronted the teacher on the school grounds, accusing her of interfering in the affairs of her family.

Further reports indicate that Lucas's life later spiraled into episodes of horrific violence, which included several murders. His detailed confession to sheriff Bill Conway triggered the largest serial-killer investigation in history. As with physical and sexual abuse, one can only assume that the emotional abuse, suffered by Lucas as a child, contributed to a dysfunctional lifestyle. This resulted in the loss of an untold number of lives left in his wake of terror. As with any perpetrator of child maltreatment, Lucas's behavior cannot be excused. However, what could the possibilities have been if there had been Christians that were providing wise counsel and strategic prayer for the Lucas family? Is it possible that Lucas's homicidal behavior could have been prevented if his family was nurtured and equipped with the Word of God in a Christian community?

Unfortunately, Lucas's behavior negatively affected many families and communities. A host of gruesome murders are attributed to Lucas and his associates. That is the reason why these indicators and dynamics are being provided in this book. You should become familiar with these factors related to emotional abuse in the following chart so that it is possible for you to help the lives of children who suffer from this maltreatment. As God's people become more sensitive to the abuses of children, they can become, "instruments of righteousness to God" (Rom. 6:13), dramatically improving lives of countless children. As children's lives are improved, the cycle of sin in families will decrease.

Figure 2-6
Emotional Abuse Indicators and Dynamics: Child
Source: South Carolina Department of Social Services[33]

Emotional Abuse	Physical Indicators: Child	Behavioral Dynamics: Child
	Lags in a child's physical development	Certain habit disorders
	Speech disorders	Biting, rocking back and forth, or sucking
	Disruptive or hyperactive behavior	Conduct or learning disorder
	Shallow or empty facial appearance	Antisocial behavior
	Child may be: • Unable to communicate • Tied or chained • Not permitted to engage in family activities • Confined to a small space	Destructive behavior
		Sleep disorders
		Neurotic traits
		Inhibition of play
		Unusual fearfulness
		Behavioral extremes
		Child may not change expressions
		Overly Compliant or Passive
		Inappropriate adult or infantile behavior
		Developmental lags
		Mental or emotional problems
		Suicide attempts

Other common family dynamics related to emotional abuse:

Family Dynamics
- Unreasonably high expectations of the abused child
- Possible substance abuse within the home
- Isolated family
- High levels of stress among family members
- Lack of bonding between parent(s) and abused child

Each incident of emotional abuse has the potential to develop another dysfunctional personality like that of Lucas. Minimizing this maltreatment while focusing on the other three could prove counterproductive in efforts to keep children and communities safe. Each of the four maltreatments deserve the full attention of both professionals and those within the Christian community. The only way to effectively combat child maltreatment is the development of a viable, effective partnership between these entities as they join forces to minimize the likelihood of child maltreatment.

Combinations of Abuse and Neglect

Many case studies of child maltreatment reveal evidence of children who have suffered from various combinations of child maltreatment. Social workers are trained to avoid developing tunnel vision when investigating alleged cases of child maltreatment. They may receive a report regarding a particular maltreatment but are to maintain an open, objective investigative demeanor, because they may uncover a situation where multiple maltreatments are present. The end result of this type of investigation is a comprehensive, qualitative assessment that will assist in ensuring the safety of children.

A contemporary case study of the effects of a child suffering from multiple maltreatments is masterfully displayed in the film titled *Antoine Fisher*. This biographical account illustrates the devastating effects that child maltreatment has on children. The story also emphasizes the development of human beings as they transition from childhood into adulthood. Fisher did not develop homicidal behavior, however; he had unresolved challenges with anger, low self-esteem, and intimacy.

The data collected by the *U.S. Department of Health and Human Services* reveals a combined percentage of 106.4% of children suffering from more than one of the maltreatments that have been discussed. This percentage number is the result of the following statement: "In 2000, 62.8 percent of victims suffered neglect (including medical neglect); 19.3 percent were physically abused; 10.1 percent were sexually abused; and 7.7 percent were emotionally or psychologically maltreated. In addition, 16.6 percent of victims were associated with "Other" types of maltreatment, which was not coded as one of the main types of maltreatment. For example, some states included "abandonment," "threats of harm to the child," and "congenital drug addiction" as "other." The percentages total more than 100 percent of victims because children may have been victims of more than one type of maltreatment."[34] With the high frequency of incidents of multiple child maltreatments being reported, investigated, and indicated, there is ample evidence for great alarm in the United States. Remember, not all cases of child maltreatment are reported and the data gathered by the *Department of Health and Human Services* is the result of dysfunctional behavior in only one country. One can only imagine what is not being reported and the magnitude of this problem worldwide.

Exemptions

Certain exemptions may vary from state to state that are applicable to the identification of child maltreatment. Most of these exemptions are couched under the category of religious exemptions. Within the parameters of these exceptions, parents are not deemed negligent if they do not seek medical care for their child(ren) if it conflicts with their religious beliefs. However, in many states, religious practices do not supercede a court order that mandates the provision of medical treatment of a child. Other exemptions exist that apply to instances of poverty, cultural variances, and forms of corporal punishment.

Knowledge That Makes A Difference

As it was in the era of the prophet Hosea, many of those today who profess Christ as Lord do not possess the biblical knowledge of the nature and character of God that is required to make a difference in the world. The story of the Good Samaritan, the healing of blind Bartemaeus, Christ's healing touch that raised Jairus's daughter from the dead, and the eternal life-giving sacrifice of the Son of God on Calvary and His resurrection provide a ringing endorsement from the Lord for the Christian community. Caring for those that are unable to care for themselves is a God-given responsibility.

The Lord is clear in His compassion for those who are hurting. The Scripture reveals the heart of God toward individuals who are in need of healing. "The Lord is near to the brokenhearted and saves those who are crushed in spirit" (Psalm 34:18) and "He heals the brokenhearted and binds up their wounds" (Psalm 147:3). God desires for those who suffer to be comforted by those who are His ambassadors here on earth. Representatives of Christ are to fulfill His wishes in providing for those that need assistance.

Mistreating children is contrary to the Word of God. In the following chapter a comparison is given showing the difference between God's initial blueprint for healthy, nurturing relationships and abusive, neglectful relationships. Chapter 3 provides insight into the manner in which the world, the flesh, and the adversary of our souls—Satan, has sought to pervert God's design for wholesome relationships. It is imperative that the Christian community access and embrace the readily available wisdom of God's Word and God-given knowledge to guard against further destruction of children.

---

[1] Lloyd Ogilvie, *The Communicator's Commentary: Hosea, Joel, Amos, Obadiah, Jonah,* (Dallas, TX, Word Books, 1990), 69.

[2] James L. Mays, *Hosea* (Philadelphia, PA, The Westminster Press), 69.

[3] Lloyd Ogilvie, *The Communicator's Commentary,* 68.

[4] Thomas L. Friedman, *The World Is Flat: A Brief History of the Twenty-First Century*, (New York, Farrar, Straus, & Giroux, 2005, 2006), 11.

[5] Jill Goldman and Marsha K. Salus, *A Coordinated Response to Child Abuse and Neglect: The Foundation for Practice*, (U.S. Department of Health and Human Services), 13.

[6] Ibid., 13.

[7] Ibid., 16.

[8] Child Welfare Information Gateway, [http://childwelfare.gov/systemwide/laws_policies/search/index.cfm], referenced 10 November, 2006.

[9] Ibid., 17–18.

[10] Ibid., 24.

[11] Ibid., 23.

[12] Maria W. Piers, *Infanticide*, (New York, Norton, 1978), 51.

[13] Douglas Linder, "*The Charles Manson Trial: A Chronology*", [http://www.law.umkc.edu/faculty/projects/ftrials/manson/mansonchrono.html], referenced 29 November 2002.

[14] Ibid., 51.

[15] *The King James Study Bible* (Nashville, TN, Thomas Nelson, 1983), 984.

[16] South Carolina Department of Social Services, Staff Development & Training: *Human Services Training Manual*, 2003.

[17] *Child Maltreatment 2000*, (Washington, D.C., U.S. Government Printing Office, United States Department of Health and Human Services, Administration on Children, Youth and Families, 2002), 4.

[18] Jill Goldman and Marsha Salus, *A Coordinated Response to Child Abuse and Neglect: The Foundation for Practice*, (U.S. Department of Health and Human Services), 16.

[19] *Child Maltreatment 2000*, 32.

[20] Newton, Michael, *Pee Wee Gaskins*, [http://www.francesfarmersrevenge.com/stuff/serialkillers/gaskins.htm], referenced 21 July 2006.

[21] South Carolina Department of Social Services, *Human Services Training Manual*, 2003.

[22] South Carolina Department of Social Services, *Human Services Training Manual*.

[23] Ibid, 14.

[24] Jill Goldman and Marsha Salus, *A Coordinated Response to Child Abuse and Neglect*, 16–17.

[25] *Child Maltreatment, 2000*, 32.

[26] Cordingley, Peter and Gee, Alison Dakota, *The Lost Children: Is There Any Hope for the Hundreds of Thousands of Asian Youngsters Trapped in the Sex Trade?*, [http://www.asiaweek.com/asiaweek/97/0207/csl.html], referenced 11 November 2006.

[27] South Carolina Department of Social Services, *Human Services Training Manual*, 2003.

[28] Ibid.

[29] Ibid., 33.

[30] Jill Goldman and Marsha K. Salus, *A Coordinated Response to Child Abuse and Neglect*, 20.

[31] Ibid, 19.

[32] Court TV Crime Library, Henry Lee Lucas: Deadly Drifter, [http://www.crimelibrary.com/serial_killers/predators/lucas/womb_2.html] referenced 31 July, 2006.

[33] South Carolina Department of Social Services, *Human Services Training Manual*, 2003.
[34] *Child Maltreatment 2000*, 24.

Chapter Three
God's Choice–Man's Blunder

"In the beginning God created…"

Genesis 1:1

Does the Bible speak to the issues of today concerning the treatment of children? If so, what examples are given in Scripture that serve as as a model for the proper treatment of God's litte ones? Where would you look first for a way to develop a model for relationships between adults and children?

Those who profess Christianity have discovered the most valuable commodity known to humanity. It is worth more than precious metals, abundant riches, and natural resources. This priceless item is none other than the Word of God. Direction needed to navigate through life is provided in these sixty-six books that make up the Bible. This book introduces us to Jesus Christ, our source of eternal life, and provides the resources to live victoriously while on earth.

Answers to a myriad of spiritual and social issues that have transcended time are found throughout Scripture. However, one of the most fundamental and foundational principles related to these issues could easily be overlooked because it occurs at the very beginning of Genesis; namely, the first five words of the Bible: "*In the beginning God created* the heavens and the earth. The earth was without form, and void; and darkness was on the face of the deep. And the Spirit of God was hovering over the face of the waters" (Gen. 1:1-2).

Before anything was created—heaven or earth, light or darkness, water or land, animal or man—God existed and then He created. He is the divine architect of all that has been developed in the universe. The first five words of Genesis reveal that the world was empty, without form, and void of everything. There were no known points of reference. We know of no previous models that were developed beforehand that would allow for duplication. For the most logical person to understand creation is difficult at best. Simply stated, God existed, and then He created all that can be seen through human lenses.

Most humans desire rational explanations and operate through deductive reasoning. As a result of this internal desire to intellectually explain causes and events, many embrace theories of evolution regarding creation because of their unbelief in God. The apostle Paul provides affirmation for the work of creation by God (described in Genesis 1) as he states in Colossians 1:16: "For by Him [Christ] all things were created that are in heaven and that are on earth, visible and invisible, whether thrones or dominions or principalities or powers. All things were created through Him and for Him." In this passage Paul writes that Christ existed before the formation of earth and played a pivotal role in the creative process. Other passages in Genesis reveal that not only did Christ play an integral role in creation, but that creation was the work of the triune God.

A Model Relationship

Gaining an understanding of creation and the work of the triune God is essential in the efforts to combat child maltreatment. It was during these formative days of the world that the divine architect, whom Christians know as the LORD, established the blueprint for godly relationships. An analysis of abuse and neglect reveals that the core issue that surrounds child maltreatment is inappropriate relationships between people as they are influenced by Satan. The relational roots of child abuse and neglect are found in the following:

- Inappropriate parent/child Relationships
- Inappropriate caregiver or stranger/child relationships; or
- Inappropriate older child/younger child relationships

A careful study of the passages in Genesis 1, along with other supporting passages, offers valuable insight into the LORD's original blueprint for human relationships. As you study the following chart, the evidence of the Triune God is obvious.

Figure 3-1
Unity of the Trinity

Scripture Reference	Unity of the Relationship Revealed
Genesis 1:1	"In the beginning **God** [Elohim] created…" **[Elohim = God the Father, Son, and Holy Spirit]**
Genesis 1:2	"…and the **Spirit of God** was hovering over the face of the waters." **[Spirit = Holy Spirit]**
Genesis 1:26	"Let **us** make man in **Our** image, according to **Our** likeness…" **[Us = God the Father, Son, & Holy Spirit]** **[Our = God the Father, Son & Holy Spirit]**
Genesis 3:22	"The man has become like one of **Us**…" **[Us = God the Father, Son, & Holy Spirit]**
Job 26:13	"By His spirit He adorned the heavens;" **[spirit = Holy Spirit]**
John 1:1-3	"In the beginning was the **Word**, and the **Word** was **with God**, and the **Word was God**. **He was in the beginning with God**. All things were made **through Him**; and **without Him nothing was made** that was made." **[Word, was, Him = Christ]**
Colossians 1:16	"For by **Him all things were created** that are in heaven and that are on earth, visible and invisible, whether thrones or dominions or principalities or powers. **All things were created through Him and for Him**." **[Him = Christ]**
Hebrews 1:2	"…has in these last days **spoken** to us **by His Son**, whom He has appointed heir of all things, **through whom also He made the worlds**;" [He = God the Father] [Son = Christ]

Scriptural evidence reveals this joint effort between God the Father, God the Son, and God the Holy Spirit in creating the universe. A careful examination of the original Hebrew language in the Old Testament shows that the word used to signify God in the afore-mentioned passages is *Elohim*. The author of Genesis used *Elohim* as a noun in the plural form. It is used not only in Genesis 1:1 but also in over 2,000 other occasions in the Old Testament. The plural usage of the term provides evidence of the cooperative nature of God. Nathan Stone suggests,

> Colossians 1:16 tells us that by Him or in Him were all things created. But creation is the act of the Elohim. Therefore, Christ is in the Elohim or Godhead. Then even in Genesis 1:3 we read that the spirit of the Elohim moved or brooded over the face of the waters. The entire creation, animate and inanimate, was, then, not only the work of the Elohim, but the object of a covenant within the Elohim guaranteeing its redemption and per-petuation. It is quite clear that the Elohim is a plurality in unity.[1]

Andrew Jukes writes,

> "First then this name, though a plural noun, when used of the one true God is constantly joined with verbs and adjectives in the singular. We are thus prepared, even from the very begin-ning, for the mystery of a plurality in God, who though He says, 'There is no God besides me,' and 'I am God, and there is none else,' says also, 'Let us make man in our image, after our like-ness'; and again, 'The man is become like one of us'; and again at Babel, 'Go to, let us go down and confound their language'; and again; in the vision granted to the prophet Isaiah, 'Whom shall I send, and who will go for us'"[2]

Further evidence of the unity and cooperative nature of *Elohim* is provided by Herbert Stevenson. Stevenson writes,

> "In the beginning God created heaven and earth. The absolute monotheism of this statement, written at a time when the peo-ples of the world believed in many gods, being the hallmark of divine self-revelation, and is one of the most striking attesta-

tions of the inspiration of the Scriptures…Elohim is a plural noun; and when God speaks, in Genesis, it is in the plural: 'Let us make man.' But the verbs used are singular, making it indisputably plain that there is no hint in the plural noun of more than one God. This is often explained as a 'plural of majesty.'"[3]

This pluralistic usage of *Elohim* suggests a relationship based on unity and cooperation within the Holy Trinity as evidenced in the formation of the world.

Some may question the relevance between the cooperative relationship exhibited by God the Father, Son, and Holy Spirit and child maltreatment. The relevance is in the respectful cohesiveness exhibited within the triune God from the beginning of creation. Their relationship illustrates unity, cooperation, singleness of vision, and relational integrity. Scripture clearly implies that no member of the Trinity took advantage of or exploited the other. They worked in perfect harmony to create the universe and continue to govern it in relational harmony and cooperation. There is a godly, relational bond between them that cannot be broken. These passages show that the LORD modeled divine solidarity for mankind to follow even before He fashioned man from the dust of the earth.

Another key element of the creative works of the Trinity is that the universe was created out of emptiness. The world was not reshaped or reformed, but established out of God's imagination. When writing the phrase "God created," the author used the Hebrew term *bara*, which means to create, instead of the term *yatsar*, which means to form or to frame. This may seem insignificant, but it is extremely important. The LORD had a specific design in mind when He created the universe. He did not refurbish previously existing blueprints but created a masterpiece from freshly inspired thoughts. Along with a fresh set of physical blueprints that formed the earth, a newly inspired mode of relational blueprints were designed that, if left untainted, would reflect the relationships that *Elohim* modeled in His creative efforts. These relational designs would reflect human relationships based on love, respect, and mutual admiration.

God's Blueprint for Human Relationships

The first two chapters in Genesis are filled with relational instructions. Nowhere in history will one ever find two people who experienced such heavenly relational bliss as Adam and Eve did during the pre-Fall era. In Genesis 1–2 when God created darkness and light, the sky and the water, the ground and the vegetation, and the living creatures in the seas, the air, and the earth, He saw that it was *good*. However, when He made man on the sixth day, He saw that the ensuing results were *very good*. The LORD's excitement over the creation of man lasted only a short period. Observing Adam's interaction with the other forms of creation, God noticed a missing element. Therefore, in Genesis 2:18 the LORD stated, "It is not good that man should be alone; I will make him a helper comparable to him." The LORD understood that there was a lack of intimacy between Adam and the rest of creation. Adam's relationship with the rest of creation was not reflective of the bond that existed between the members of the Trinity. Therefore, God stated: "I will make him a helper comparable to him." A dog may be man's best friend but that does not make it a *comparable* helper.

According to Stanley Grenz, the Hebrew word *ezer* is used to describe the word "helper" in this passage. *Ezer* refers to one who saves or delivers. Grenz writes, "God's desire, therefore, was to create another human being who would deliver Adam from his solitude by being a suitable bonding partner for him, not merely sexual, but in all dimensions of existence."[4] It was the LORD's desire to create a partner for Adam so there would be mutual love, respect, and cooperation as modeled by the Trinity. This does not imply some type of mystical, cosmic sexual relationship within the Holy

Trinity, but one of close divine intimacy that illustrates a genuine love, respect, and adoration for one another that supersedes any type of physical intimacy. Only in the formation of Eve would Adam find one who could save or deliver him from the emotional isolation that he must have felt in the Garden. The LORD knew that only this type of relationship would provide the abundant fruit that He so desired man to produce.

The creation of godly generations and godly relationships are evidence of the abundant fruit that the LORD envisioned. This is the relational blueprint that God longed for from the beginning; one that would be transferred from one generation to the next. No other element found in creation could meet the criteria of a *comparable* helper for Adam. When the LORD created Eve, He did not form her from the "dust of the ground" (Gen. 2:7), as He did with Adam. Instead, God put Adam into a deep sleep, took one of his ribs from his side, and fashioned a *comparable* helper. She came from the bones of Adam's bones, and the flesh of Adam's flesh. The LORD sought a type of relational closeness for Adam and Eve in such a manner that they would be a perfect fit. A picture of this level of relational intimacy is seen in Genesis 2:24: "Therefore a man shall leave his father and mother and be *joined to his wife*, and they shall become *one flesh*." God established the marital covenant as a continuation of His biblical blueprint for relationships. This covenant was one of holiness, integrity, honor, faithfulness, and respect. It would serve as a symbolic representation of the relationship between Jesus Christ and His believers as the prophet Isaiah stated: "For your *Maker* is your *husband*, The LORD of hosts is His name; and your Redeemer is the Holy One of Israel; He is called the God of the whole earth" (Isaiah 54:5).

Men and women enter into a covenant relationship with one another on their wedding day. The LORD has a purpose to work through married couples. Symbolically, they serve as salt and light to the world illustrating Christ's love for His people. The Apostle Paul wrote about this symbolic relationship to the church at Ephesus:

> submitting to one another in the fear of God.
>
> Wives, submit to your own husbands, as to the LORD. For the husband is head of the wife, as also Christ is head of the church; and He is the Savior of the body. Therefore, just as the church is subject to Christ, so let the wives be to their own husbands in everything.
>
> Husbands, love your wives, just as Christ also loved the church and gave Himself for her, that He might sanctify and cleanse her with the washing of water by the word, that He might present her to Himself a glorious church, not having spot or wrinkle or any such thing, but that she should be holy and without blemish. So husbands ought to love their own wives as their own bodies; he who loves his wife loves himself. For no one ever hated his own flesh, but nourishes and cherishes it, just as the LORD does the church. For we are members of His body, of His flesh and of His bones. *"For this reason a man shall leave his father and mother and be joined to his wife, and the two shall become one flesh."* This is a great mystery, but I speak concerning Christ and the church."
>
> Ephesians 5:21-32

As previously stated, the LORD's blueprint for relationships consists of a godly affection between a husband (man) and wife (woman), which should be taught to every generation. This blueprint also includes the mutual respect and honor for those who are single. Numerous passages in Scripture refer to the LORD's expectations regarding the care and treatment of all of mankind. One passage summarizes each of these commands regarding relationships. It is considered to be one of Christ's greatest commandments as it is found in three of the four gospel accounts:

Jesus said to him, 'You shall love the LORD your God with all your heart, with all your soul, and with all your mind.' This is the first and great commandment. And the second is like it: 'You shall love your neighbor as yourself.' On these two commandments hang all the Law and the Prophets.

Matthew 22:37-40

The design for godly relationships was modeled in the creation of the universe. Man was then fashioned in His image and likeness so that humans could reflect the same relational characteristics exhibited by the Trinity. With God's design being developed upon these spiritual tenets, how did man's behavior digress to the level where approximately one million annual cases of child abuse and neglect are reported? How was the original relational blueprint perverted?

Perverting the Blueprint

God's original design for people is clear in the Scripture. Man and woman were not created for the purpose of conflict. They were created by God to be helpful, loving companions. Husband and wife were to procreate and raise children in a model environment. Satan, however, had a different plan. His methods of deceit and hate would be the very base for child maltreatment.

Christians are not unaware of Satan's schemes as they rely on God's Word to expose his tactics. The book of Mark helps to unfold a pattern of Satan that has transcended time and provides insight into his efforts to undermine the LORD's original plans for the family. Mark 4:15 states: "And these are the ones by the wayside where the word is sown. When they hear, Satan comes immediately and takes away the word that was sown in their hearts." One of the most observable patterns of Satan is that he will attempt to immediately corrupt what the LORD has blessed. Satan's intentions are to stop people from receiving salvation or the ability to live victoriously while on earth.

Adam and Eve were corrupted in a similar way. Genesis 2:25 reveals that Adam and Eve "...were naked, yet felt no shame." Human sin did not exist at this time, so Adam and Eve were not embarrassed by their nakedness. However, Genesis 3:1 reveals a divisive wedge that destroyed their perfect union: "Now the serpent was the most cunning of all the wild animals that the LORD God had made. He said to the woman, "Did God really say, 'You can't eat from any tree in the garden'?" Satan delights in polluting God's workmanship. Adam and Eve fell prey to the temptation of Satan soon after they received instructions from God. This altered the LORD's blueprint for godly relationships. Genesis 2:7 reveals this truth: "Then the LORD God formed the man out of the dust from the ground and breathed the breath of life into his nostrils, and the man became a living being." As a result of their disobedience, Adam and Eve understood both "good and evil" (Gen. 3:22). The godly relationship between man and woman, that was once centered on love, respect, and unity, was now replaced with pleasure seeking and self-centeredness that has carried on through generations and remains a part of society in the twenty-first century.

Genesis chapter four provides additional evidence of this radical shift in relational behavior. Cain committed the first act of murder against his brother Abel. God had established a perfect relationship. Now, the enemy had come to quickly "steal and to kill and to destroy" (John 10:10). The results of Satan's efforts became real and personal in the literal destruction of human life. Those early relationships that were based upon love and respect were now substituted by those of exploitation, manipulation, and destruction. This was the beginning of human maltreatment.

Having an understanding of God's original plan for human relationships is crucial. Now as efforts are made to assist those that have suffered from child maltreatment, and local agencies have been commissioned to spearhead these efforts, there should be a better understanding of the need to address the spiritual component of the battle. The need for spiritual assistance is evident and should be viewed as an integral part of the solution. It is only the coupling of biblical insight with the knowledge of the intricacies of child maltreatment that equips the Christian community to effectively partner with local child protective services and law enforcement to strategically combat abuse and neglect. The following will further strengthen the scriptural foundation for relationships by examining other relevant passages that directly oppose the four maltreatments discussed in the previous chapter.

Godly Nurturing vs. Neglect

Jesus illustrated physical nurturing in John 14:2 when He said, "In my Father's house are many mansions; if it were not so, I would have told you. I am going there to prepare a place for you. And if I go and prepare a place for you, I will come back and take you to be with me that you also may be where I am."

James Hatch provides insight into this passage in his series on godly blueprints for parenting. Hatch stated that God has prepared a place for His children in these mansions. These mansions are places of rest where the children of God will dwell without fear of hurt, harm, or danger. As Christ instructed the disciples on prayer in Matthew 6:9–13 He stated in verse 10, "Your [God the Father] kingdom come. Your [God the Father] will be done on earth as it is in heaven." Hatch stated that if the will of the LORD is going to be accomplished here on earth as it is in heaven, then the perfect place of rest and protection for each child is the home. Homes should reflect what the Father has prepared for Christians in heaven (i.e., a safe, nurturing, protective environment).

Many home environments do not resemble places of rest. Unfortunately, through the eyes of some children, their home environments simulate war zones. Children need to feel safe, secure, and at rest when in their home environment. Parents and caregivers are to provide this kind of home.

Scriptural assurance that the Father in heaven has a never-ending love and attentiveness when it comes to caring for His children is described in Hebrews 13:5. The LORD states, "I will never leave you or forsake you." But just what does Jesus Christ do to fulfill this promise? After His death, resurrection, and ascension, He sent His Spirit, the Holy Spirit, the Comforter, to be with those who accept Him as Savior and LORD. The Holy Spirit dwells within each Christian. He is there to lead, guide, correct, and direct them as they navigate through life.

Parents and caregivers can use this example to enhance their parenting skills. Human Service professionals use the term *best practice* to describe the best methods or methodologies in addressing specific situations. The example given in Hebrews 13:5 is the biblical *best practice* for parents. This model speaks against physical neglect. The Bible documents that the Father sent His Son to save sinners from eternal damnation; the Son in turn sent the Holy Spirit to dwell within and to care for those who convert to Christianity, while the Son went to heaven to prepare places of rest for them. Regardless of what people may think, believers have never been, nor will they ever be, left alone here on earth.

It is essential to develop a brief profile for neglectful parents or caregivers. Public perception many times is that the neglectful parent or caregiver is usually a single person living on pubic welfare. This is far from reality. Neglectful parents are found in all socio-economic classes. Children are physically neglected in many two-parent homes. Parents are usually consumed with their own personal agendas, professions, social activities, and friends. Sometimes they give so much time to the local church while neglecting quality time with their children. The home environment feels as empty to children as it would if their parents were bodily absent from the home. Rarely, if ever, would a report of this type be considered a case of neglect. However, the ramifications upon the child are still damaging if the situation persists over an extended period of time.

Deuteronomy 4:9 is relevant to this issue: "Only take heed to yourself, and diligently keep yourself, lest you forget the things your eyes have seen, and lest they depart from your heart all the days of your life. And teach them to your children and your grand-children." The LORD blesses parents and caregivers with the privilege of nurturing children who are equipped with little more than the capacity to learn. They enter into the world with limited knowledge and, as a result of the events in the Garden of Eden, a sinful nature. Children have a need to be taught how to develop into productive citizens, and it is the responsibility of parents and caregivers to accomplish this task. Parents and caregivers are responsible for teaching their children in a safe environment. This assignment to teach their children is given by God. Quality time has to be scheduled during the course of the day for their children. When neglect occurs, parents and caregivers act in an irresponsible manner. In essence, physical neglect allows the world, the flesh, and the devil to serve as surrogate parents for children.

Proverb 22:6 provides a timeless biblical principle: "Train up a child in the way he should go, and when he is old he will not depart from it." If parents unite and focus on training their children in a godly manner, they increase the likelihood that their little ones will grow up to be all that God created them to be. If the call to parenting, which takes a tremendous amount of time and energy, is not taken seriously, then parents fail in the duties that have been assigned to them by the LORD. In addition, they fail to equip the world leaders of tomorrow.

Emotional Support vs. Emotional Abuse

Most people have witnessed emotional abuse either in the family of someone with whom they are acquainted or in their own family. Why individuals emotionally abuse children is difficult to understand. Abusers have many excuses for why they act as they do toward children. Many abusers tend to rationalize their behavior by describing it as "good old-fashioned" discipline. Their methods are similar to those of military drill instructors. These methods are designed to break the spirit of a recruit so that a new foundation can be laid and a preferred mindset engrained into their psyche.

A helpful question to pose regarding emotional abuse is, "Are these forms of discipline motivated by love or by anger?" More than likely, they are birthed and ultimately manifested out of anger and poor coping skills. This is contradictory to the Word of God and how He disciplines His children. In Hebrews 12:5-6 the LORD shares His underlying motivation regarding discipline: "My son, do not despise the chastening of the LORD, Nor be discouraged when you are rebuked by Him; for whom the LORD loves He chastens, and scourges every son whom He receives."

Whenever Christians are disciplined by the LORD, it is done out of love and compassion, not anger. However convicting the discipline may be, those being disciplined should be reminded that if God did not love them, He would allow them to continue in rebellion to His Word and risk eternal damnation. Christians represent God's lineage; therefore, He would do nothing to destroy them, only to correct and transform them into His image. Believers often need to be reminded that God's form of discipline is not a form of punishment, but correction. God the Father desires to mold believers into the image of His Son, Jesus Christ, so that they can maximize their potential while on earth.

Establishing a nurturing relationship between parent and child is one of the most important components in alleviating emotional abuse. This is an area where secular child psychologists agree with Scripture. Psychologists understand that if parents and caregivers do not have a nurturing relationship with the children who they care for, then the child(ren) may be robbed of their humanity and spiral into a steady stream of dysfunctional behavior. When parents are involved in the lives of children and discipline them out of love, they please the LORD and He blesses their efforts. Such love produces children who later appreciate the disciplining efforts of their parents and share that same love with the next generation.

Two passages give insight to the will of God in this particular area. Ephesians 6:4 states, "And you, fathers, do not provoke your children to wrath, but bring them up in the training and admonition of the LORD." A similar passage is Colossians 3:21, "Fathers, do not provoke your children, lest they become discouraged." Although the apostle Paul addresses fathers in these passages, the principle applies to all caregivers. He is encouraging each believer not to badger or constantly berate children, as it could potentially result in severe emotional damage.

In the New Testament the Greek words *paideuo* and *paideia* are used to refer to the disciplining of a person (Luke 23:16; Luke 23:22, 1 Tim. 1:20). It is no coincidence that these same words are also used to refer to the nurturing that occurs in families where discipline and instruction are corrective actions administered by parents behavior (Acts 7:22; Heb. 12:6-7; Heb. 12:10; 1 Cor. 11:32; 2 Cor. 6:9; Rev. 3:19). The LORD's method of discipline is birthed out of a desire to nurture His children through loving, corrective discipline. Therefore, His *best practice* for rearing healthy children has already been established in Scripture. By following God's pattern of disciplining children, parents will not exasperate or discourage them as they grow through their formative years.

Biblical Discipline vs. Physical Abuse

Robert McGee writes that there are two reasons that children require discipline: "to teach and to warn."[5] The first reason, "to teach," has already been examined. "To warn" will now be examined.

Children encounter a number of dangers throughout their childhood that require constant warnings from parents and caregivers. Sometimes children respond to the warnings appropriately, while at other times they continue acting out, engaging in potentially self-destructive behaviors. Genesis 8:21 provides insight into the spiritual condition of children: "...the imagination of man's heart is evil from his youth; [childhood]". Even the heart of a child is in a sinful condition. This sinful state is identical to that of the unredeemed heart of adults. Regardless of innocent appearance, without Christ as their Savior and LORD, the hearts of children are unredeemed and evil.

The psalmist wrote in Psalm 51:5, "Behold, I was brought forth in iniquity, and in sin my mother conceived me." As he wrote this Psalm, David recognized his need for redemption and discipline from the earliest stages of infancy. Without the guiding hand of his father, Jesse, David would have likely committed even more sins, resulting in far greater consequences than those that are recorded in Scripture. It is because of this sinful state that children need godly nurturing and discipline through guiding cautions and admonishment. Through these warnings, children progress through childhood and minimize destructive behaviors. Without this guidance, they are left to the guiding hand of the adversary.

Godly Discipline (Correction vs. Punishment)

The LORD's method of discipline is twofold: to instruct and to correct. Parents and caregivers are expected to provide these disciplinary measures of correction in a manner that does not cause serious injury to children. In many instances children are injured as the result of physical abuse when their parents or caregivers respond inappropriately. These injuries are often caused by fatigue, a loss of patience, substance abuse, poor coping skills, or dysfunctional behavior. The results of these poor decisions can be devastating. God provided clear disciplinary guidelines in His Word. He illustrates the necessity of discipline while focusing on loving correction, not punitive measures resulting from anger and rage.

There are several forms of discipline that are biblically acceptable and fall within the federal parameters of appropriate discipline. These forms of discipline include:

- **Consequences for behaviors** (ex. Isaiah 14:12: "How you have fallen from heaven, O morning star, son of the dawn! You have been cast down to the earth"–Satan was cast out of heaven for trying to assume the place of God Almighty.)

- **Loss of privileges** (ex. Genesis 3:24: "The LORD God banished Adam from the Garden of Eden to work the ground from which he had been taken."–Adam and Eve were removed from the Garden of Eden for their disobedience).

- **Physical Labor** (ex. Genesis 3:17: "Cursed is the ground because of you; In toil you will eat of it all the days of your life."–Adam was called to physical labor for his disobedience.

- **Corporal Punishment** (Spanking) (ex. Proverb 13:24: He who spares the rod hates his son, but he who loves him is careful to discipline him"; Proverb 29:15: "the rod of correction imparts wisdom, but a child left to himself shames his mother"–These are general principles regarding the use of corporal punishment in the disciplining process. The "rod of correction" is a form of discipline, not license to injure.)[6]

These Scriptures reveal the LORD'S will pertaining to proper care for children that does not risk physical injury. Appropriate nurturing is required to help children reach their full potential and become productive citizens in society. The biblical approach to discipline prevents cycles of abuse and neglect while many non-biblical forms of discipline perpetuate a vicious trend of physical injury that can be passed from one generation to the next. Through appropriate biblical behavior modification, children mature with respect for their parents, other caregivers, and those in positions of authority. Later in life they will respect and honor those who provided godly discipline, and in many occasions will offer thanks to them. Hebrews 12 illustrates this in verse 11: "Now no chastening seems to be joyful for the present, but painful; nevertheless, afterward it yields the peaceable fruit of righteousness to those who have been trained by it." Children never enjoy discipline. Correction seldom produces shouts of joy. However, as children mature into adulthood and gain an understanding of the love in which the discipline was administered, they develop an appreciation for the effort that their parents and caregivers took to correct undesirable behavior.

The unpleasant results of improper discipline could include stints in prison, substance abuse, or even death. As children grow into adulthood, they observe the pitfalls that may have overcome some of their friends. They will be grateful for the corrective attention they received in their formative years that prevented them from venturing down similar paths.

Hatch offers a biblical analogy from 1 Samuel that is relevant to the appropriate discipline of children. He makes a comparison between Samuel and the sons of Eli and the vast difference in the parenting styles under which they were raised. Samuel's parents, Elkanah and Hannah, taught him to worship and serve the LORD (1 Sam. 1:28). Eli's children were priests who sinned (2:17-22) against God and were never disciplined for their transgressions. Samuel and Eli's sons were raised in the time frame of the book of Judges.

During this era men lived abominable lives because the children of Israel had not destroyed the inhabitants of the Promised Land; the Israelites' offspring were now being exposed to sinful lifestyles of these people. Elkanah and Hannah made a positive difference in Samuel's life because of appropriate parenting. Eli failed in his parenting. As a result 1 Samuel 2:12 states, "Now the sons of Eli were corrupt; they did not know the LORD."

Unfortunately, in too many instances parents do not care for their children as Elkanah and Hannah cared for Samuel. Godly discipline must not be neglected or replaced with ungodly discipline. Ungodly discipline can have destructive results. Those forms of discipline that cause physical injury to children are not approved by the LORD but are, conversely, schemes of the devil. The only remedy for those who physically abuse children is to report them to the proper authorities, educate them on the appropriate methods of discipline, and help them develop an intimate relationship with the LORD in order that they may understand the biblical principles of godly relationships and discipline.

Intimacy: Appropriate vs. Inappropriate

During a Sunday morning service, Pastor Stephen Chitty stated, "one of the best indicators of a society's moral values is its level of sexual sin or perversion."[7] Members of the congregation were led to reflect on the level of immorality that has overtaken American society in the twenty-first century. In the year 2000 there were over 87,000 cases of sexual abuse reported in the United States, and only the LORD knows how many thousands of other cases were unreported.

Where then do the citizens of the United States rate on God's moral scale? As children are sold, exploited, and forced into prostitution around the globe, how does twenty-first-century society rate morally? It is difficult to imagine Sodom and Gomorrah being much worse than today's society. It is even more difficult to fathom why there is an absence of global outcry to denounce and strategically combat the injustices against children. The severity of sentencing the perpetrators of sexual abuse and other forms of child abuse and neglect should be increasing.

God's design for appropriate sexual intimacy is relatively simple. Scripture describes sexual relations outside of a marriage between one man and one woman as sin. Those who try to rationalize sexual intimacy outside of the biblical parameters are rejecting the scriptural model and are therefore rejecting God. Human beings are never closer or more intimate than during sexual intimacy. The sexual union between a husband and wife is symbolic of the closeness that the LORD wants with every believer. This desire for closeness is not to imply that the LORD wants a sexual relationship with humans. He desires a spiritual connection, built upon love and admiration, that is just as intimate as the sexual union between a husband and wife. At this level of intimacy, the LORD's followers are sharing all facets of their lives with Him. The apostle John describes such intimacy in Revelation 7:9-12:

> After these things I looked, and behold, a great multitude which no one could number, of all nations, tribes, peoples, and tongues, standing before the throne and before the Lamb, clothed with white robes, with palm branches in their hands, and crying out with a loud voice, saying, "Salvation belongs to our God who sits on the throne, and to the Lamb!" All the angels stood around the throne and the elders and the four living creatures, and fell on their faces before the throne and worshiped God, saying: "Amen! Blessing and glory and wisdom, Thanksgiving and honor and power and might, Be to our God forever and ever. Amen."

This passage provides a glimpse of what is to come in heaven. The scene depicts an intimate connection between the Creator and creation. It describes a countless multitude of all nations and tribes worshipping and adoring God Almighty. The *Wesleyan Bible Commentary* offers an explanation of this forthcoming event as it states, "the innumerable multitude before the throne serves to complete the heavenly assembly in chapters 4 and 5...they are also described as those who come out of great tribulation and who washed their robes, and made them white in the blood of the Lamb."[8] Standing before the LORD is an assembly of Christians from every generation since the world was created, paying homage to their King. The promise made to the patriarchs of the Christian church in the book of Genesis (13:16; 15:5; 32:12) is finally fulfilled as glorious praises are sung to the LORD. The author is seeing a vision of a family that has been brought together for the first time–in glorious celebration, in a spirit of unanimity, and in one purpose: worshipping God.

God also desires the kind of intimacy described in Genesis 2:18, when the LORD created Adam and stated,"It is not good that man should be alone; I will make him a helper comparable to him." Even though Adam was surrounded by all of God's creation, God knew that nothing that had been created was appropriate for Adam. Therefore, in Genesis 2:20 the LORD shared that out of all that was created before, "there was not found a helper comparable to him." The origin of the word *helper* (*ezer*) comes from the Hebrew word *azer*. This word does not imply subordination of the woman to the man, but one who saves or delivers.[9] It is also used in the Psalms to refer to the LORD as man's helper. The LORD instructed Adam, that there is only one who is suitable to serve as an intimate companion for him. That companion would be Eve, who was fashioned out of the flesh of her companion. Eve was created to save Adam from social isolation. The supernatural, purposeful creation of Eve from the rib of Adam is solidified in verse 24, as the Scripture states,

"Therefore a man shall leave his father and mother and be joined to his wife, and they shall become one flesh." The LORD's intentions are that nothing other than their individual relationships with Him should replace the level of intimacy that a husband and a wife experience together.

Another biblical principle regarding intimacy is found in Genesis 2:25. Sexual purity and integrity are illustrated as this passage states, "And they were both naked, the man and his wife, and were not ashamed." As previously stated, sin had not yet entered into the world, so there was no need for shame between Adam and Eve as they interacted with each other in their nakedness. The LORD's original design was uncorrupted; it was pure and full of integrity. His design was without blemish and without any perverted thoughts about intimacy. However, Satan immediately recognized how this pure relationship would expedite his demise and seized the opportunity to delay it by tempting Eve. If the chapter indicators between chapters two and three were removed and the passage was read as a continuing sequence of events, it would show that Satan instantly tempted Adam and Eve in an effort to disrupt the sexual integrity and intimacy that they shared. Seven verses after they were tempted, the two become ashamed of their nakedness and begin scheming with a threefold plan: 1) they sought a way to cover up their flesh, 2) they sought to find a place to hide from the LORD, and 3) they sought a scapegoat to cast blame for their weakness.

Pedophiles also try to cover up their offenses when caught. Many of them blame others for their dysfunctional behavior instead of taking responsibility for their actions.

Recognizing the damage done by man's disobedience, the LORD gave specific instructions to a fallen human race in regard to sexual intimacy in Leviticus 18. God's intent was to lay a foundation that would serve as a guide to correct the perversion of intimacy. A review of these verses in Leviticus provides a better understanding of the heart of the LORD regarding sexual relations.

Figure 3-2
Biblical Guidelines For Sexual Intimacy–Leviticus 18

Leviticus 18
v.6 "No one is to approach any close relative to have sexual relations. I am the LORD." **[denounces acts of incest]**
v. 7 "Do not dishonor your father by having sexual relations with you mother. She is your mother; do not have relations with her" **[denounces sexual relations between mothers and their children]**
v. 8 "Do not have sexual relations with your father's wife; that would dishonor your father." **[denounces sexual relations between step-mothers and children]**
v. 9 "Do not have sexual relations with your sister, either your father's daughter or your mother's daughter, whether she is born in the same home or elsewhere." **[denounces sexual relations between a half sister and a half sibling in the home]**
v. 10 "Do not have sexual relations with your son's daughter or your daughter's daughter; that would dishonor you." **[denounces sexual relations between grandparents and grandchildren]**
v. 11 "Do not have sexual relations with the daughter of your father's wife, born to your father; she is your sister." **[denounces sexual relations between stepsisters and another stepsibling in the home]**
v. 12 "Do not have sexual relations with you father's sister; she is your father's close relative." **[denounces sexual relations between paternal aunts and nieces and nephews]**
v. 13 "Do not have sexual relations with your mother's sister because she is your mother's close relative." **[denounces sexual relations between maternal aunts and nieces and nephews]**
v. 14 "Do not dishonor your father's brother by approaching his wife to have sexual relations; she is your aunt." **[again denounces the sexual relations between paternal aunts and nieces and nephews]** v. 15 "Do not have sexual relations with your daughter-in-law. She is your son's wife: do not have relations with her." **[denounces sexual relations between parents and daughters-in-laws]**
v. 16 "Do not have sexual relations with your brother's wife: that would dishonor your brother." **[denounces sexual adulterous relations between in-laws]**
v. 17 "Do not have sexual relations with both a woman and her daughter. Do not have sexual relations with either her son's daughter or her daughter's daughter: they are her close relatives. That is wickedness." **[denounces sexual relations with the daughter or granddaughter of a woman whom you are involved with]**

Leviticus 18 (cont'd)

v. 18 "Do not take your wife's sister as a rival wife and have sexual relations with her while your wife is living."
[denounces sexual relations between a man and his sister-in-law]

v. 19 "Do not approach a woman to have sexual relations during the uncleanness of her monthly period."
[denounces sexual relations with a woman during her menstrual cycle]

v. 20 "Do not have sexual relations with your neighbor's wife and defile yourself with her."
[denounces adultery with a neighbor's wife]

v. 22 "Do not lie with a man as one lies with a woman; that is detestable."
[denounces homosexual sexual relations]

These passages reflect the heart of the LORD regarding sexual intimacy. They speak against any form of sexual activity outside of the covenant of marriage between a man and a woman. God's heart is further revealed in surrounding passages. The LORD spoke to Moses regarding the defilement of the land by those who practiced such wicked sexuality. He commanded Moses and the Israelites that they must obey His laws. Several passages are devoted to warnings and consequences attached to the evils of sexual immorality. They provide clear instructions regarding how the perverted blueprint for sexual intimacy could be restored. Unfortunately, many have not adhered to the Word of the LORD and have consequently reaped a harvest that includes the continual perversion and exploitation of children.

The relational blueprints established by the LORD transcend time and are as relevant today as they were thousands of years ago. The results of deviating from these plans often manifest themselves in cases of child maltreatment. Depending upon the individual, the developmental consequences vary. The effects of these maltreatments are examined in the chapter 4.

[1] Nathan Stone, *Names of God*, (Chicago, IL, Moody Press, 1944), 15.

[2] Andrew Jukes, *The Names of God In Holy Scripture*, (Grand Rapids, MI, Kregel, 1976), 16.

[3] Herbert F. Stevenson, *Titles of the Triune God*, (Westwood, NJ, Revell, 1956), 7–9.

[4] Stanley Grenz, *Sexual Ethics: A Biblical Perspective*, (Dallas, TX, Word, 1990), 19.

[5] Robert McGee, *Discipline With Love*, (Dallas, TX, Word, 1990), 2.

[6] Mental Health Journal, *Child Abuse: An Overview–Child Physical Abuse and Corporal Punishment*, [http://www.therpistfinder.net/Child-Abuse/Corporal-Punishment.html], referenced 14 November 2006.

[7] Stephen Chitty, "*Why Sexual Sins Are More Damaging Than Others*" (Sermon, Christian Life Assemblies of God Church, Columbia, S.C., 10 March, 1998).

[8] Charles W. Carter, *The Wesleyan Bible Commentary* (Grand Rapids, MI, Eerdman's Publishing, 1966), 452.

[9] Stanley Grenz, *Sexual Ethics*, 19.

Chapter Four
An Unmeasureable Cost

"...and you may be sure that your sin will find you out."
Num. 32:23

In the book of Numbers, Moses warned the Israelites about the consequences of their sin. He could not have possibly imagined how relevant his warning would be to us thousands of years after his death. Those who sin are often led into a false sense of security if their sin was not done in public or immediately brought to light. "In many ways sinners practice deceit on themselves and harden themselves in iniquity. Men are not done with sin when they have committed it. After sin comes a dread account."[1] Regardless of the severity of the sin, the consequences are never hidden from the Lord and in many instances are brought to light in the public eye. The following categories suggest ways in which this occurs.

I. God certainly shows His purpose to punish sin by the way He causes woe to come on some sinners here...Men may plot very secretly, and think their crimes are hidden, but Providence calls on stones and beams of timber, on tracks and pieces of paper, to be witnesses of the crime.

II. Men might be sure that their sin will find them out by sore judgments which God sometimes sends on men for their sins...Look at the history of Achan, of Korah...Of thirty Roman Emperors, Proconsuls, and high officials, who distinguished themselves by their zeal and rage against early Christians, it is recorded that one became speedily deranged

93

after an act of great cruelty; one was slain by his own son; one became blind; the eyes of one started out of his head; one was drowned, etc.

III. One may escape detection and strange judgments, and still his sins may find him out in the fears, and clamours, and remorse of conscience...Remorse is remorseless. Like fire, it burns all around it. No man can protect himself against his sins flashing him in the face at any moment.

IV. But even if one escape all these things, yet if he dies unpardoned his sins will find him out in the next world...O sinner, "be sure your sin will find you out." You may now live in ease and in error. You may now harden your heart in pride. But you must meet your sins at God's tribunal. Remember that. O be wise unto salvation.–W. S. Plumer, D.D.[2]

The offenses against children, which directly oppose the commands of the Lord, continue to have a devastating impact upon our society, both relationally and economically. Members of society can rest assured that the Scriptures are indeed true; the sins related to child maltreatment are being revealed in a number of areas. How interesting it is that in verse 24 of that chapter Moses gives commands to build protective fortresses for the "little ones." Even he understood how important it is to properly care for children.

The case study of Diana and her older brother, John, offers a glimpse of the impact of abuse and neglect on children. Diana shared the following information during an interview in 2003. She revealed that she and her brother were born to a couple in the mid 1970s who would eventually abandon them at their childcare center. No family member ever returned to pick them up, and they were taken into protective custody. Diana and John were fortunate enough to be placed with the same foster parents; however, the lives of the siblings took radically different paths. Diana shared that many of the memories she experienced as she grew up in the home of "momma" and "daddy" (the foster parents) were happy ones. She remembers being active in church and school, which made her feel welcome in their home. She never felt like an outsider that was intruding the personal space of her foster family. John also experienced few problems and he maintained an active role in their church. According to Diana, John did well when he was involved with the church but his behavior worsened whenever he wasn't participating in church activities.

The major turning point in their lives came when their foster mother passed away. She and John remained with their foster family (much to the chagrin of some of the foster parents' biological family members), but their young lives would never be the same. They had difficulties adjusting, as their foster mother was the only sense of stability they had ever known. Diana adjusted over time, but John never did. He struggled with another loss in his life and found it difficult to adapt. He began to spiral downward, exhibiting a pattern of incorrigible behavior. This resulted in numerous interventions by the local social service agency, visits to physicians, and sessions with school counselors. John eventually left home and never had the opportunity to share the formative years of development with his sister.

Diana continued to develop normally, while John transitioned in and out of several different placements (i.e., foster homes, group homes, etc.) and eventual stints in the *Department of Juvenile Justice*. According to Diana, "John never benefited from all of the psychologists and psychiatrists that were involved with his life." John's behavior worsened as he became involved with gangs, got involved in numerous physical altercations, and began using drugs. He also began to mistreat the women in his life and tried to commit suicide more times than Diana can remember. John's life continued the downward spiral, and he ended up serving time in an adult correctional institution. Diana, however, successfully graduated from high school and college. She married and currently works as a social worker in a child protective services agency, seeking to help those who are experiencing circumstances similar to those that she and her brother experienced as children. Diana often reflects on her childhood and how she and her brother handled their circumstances in different ways.

This story is not uncommon among siblings. It illustrates the challenges of caring for children who have been abused or neglected. It also illustrates one of the principles being emphasized in this book. If members of society are to effectively engage child maltreatment, then effective partnerships must be developed between the Christian community and public services for children. This partnership increases the likelihood of success for children who have suffered due to abuse or neglect.

Following is an examination of three major areas related to the impact of child maltreatment and how each member of society is impacted either directly or indirectly by this sin. The three areas are: the impact on taxpayers, the impact upon society, and the impact upon children and families. The sins related to child maltreatment are being brought to light to illustrate Numbers 32:23. No longer can society hide behind the cloak of ignorance and indifference. The sins of nations have been "found out." Those who have never been exposed to abuse or neglect may wonder how this could possibly impact them. A critical look at the first area offers evidence of the far-reaching impact of this issue and how it affects each tax-paying citizen.

Financial Impact

In April of 2001, an astonishing report was published by the organization *Prevent Child Abuse America*. The report documented both the direct costs (those associated with the immediate needs of abused and neglected children) and the indirect costs (those associated with the longer term and secondary effects of child maltreatment) of child abuse and neglect in the United States. It is estimated that this sin issue costs United States taxpayers a staggering $94 billion every year. That is an estimated $258 million per day spent in the United States alone on a problem widely ignored by most citizens. What is even more perplexing is that the staff of *Prevent Child Abuse America* estimates that these figures are conservative because of the stringent standards set by the *United States Department of Health and Human Services* as the data was collected. According to *Prevent Child Abuse*, other costs were not included, such as the provision of welfare benefits to adults whose economic condition is often a result of the abuse and neglect they suffered as children.

Figure 4-1

Total Daily Cost of Child Abuse and Neglect in the United States[3]

Direct Costs	Estimated Daily Costs
Health Care System	
Hospitalization	$17,001,082
Chronic Health Problems	8,186,185
Mental Health Care System	1,164,686
Child Welfare System	39,454,054
Law Enforcement	67,698
Judicial System	934,725
Total Direct Costs	**$66,806,430**
Indirect Costs	
Special Education	$612,624
Mental Health and Health Care	12,678,455
Juvenile Delinquency	24,124,086
Adult Criminality	151,726,027
Total Indirect Costs	**$190,938, 452**
Total Daily Costs	**$257,744,882**

Figure 4-2

Total Annual Costs of Child Abuse and Neglect in the United States[4]

Direct Costs	Estimated Annual Costs
Health Care System	
Hospitalization	$6,205,395,000
Chronic Health Problems	2,987,957,400
Mental Health Care System	425,110,400
Child Welfare System	14,400,000,000
Law Enforcement	24,709,800
Judicial System	341,174,702
Total Daily Costs	**$24,384,347,302**

Indirect Costs	Estimated Annual Costs
Special Education	$223,607,830
Mental Health and Health Care	4,627,636,025
Juvenile Delinquency	8,85,291,372
Lost Productivity to Society	656,000,000
Adult Criminality	55,380,000,000
Total Annual Indirect Costs	**69,692,535,227**
Total Annual Costs	**$94,076,882,529**

The data gathered by *Prevent Child Abuse* provides evidence of the overwhelming impact that child maltreatment has on each tax-paying citizen in the United States. Billions of dollars are spent addressing the maltreatment of children annually. These funds could be disbursed into other areas of society to help maintain a strong economy; yet, they are being distributed to address a problem that does not receive adequate national attention. Remember, those who gathered these statistics estimate that the data collected represents conservative figures. These figures should serve as a catalyst to raise the level of concern of those who belong to the work force in America. They are essentially paying $258 million per day towards a national problem that is not being addressed effectively. These figures should be a focal topic of discussion before, during, and after each election. Political officials should assist citizens in establishing a level of local and national accountability that will reduce the necessity of spending $94 billion per year.

Unfortunately, the deceptive nature of Satan is evident in the political system and in the skirmishes related to partisanship. If the enemy of our souls did not have many deceived, there would be more elected officials willing to address the needs of children. There would also be those with the political and spiritual where-withal to embrace biblical principles and apply them to their efforts in public service. C. S. Lewis captures the essence of the deceptive nature of Satan as it relates to Christianity, politics, and social justice as he writes:

> The "historical Jesus," then, however dangerous he may seem to be to us at some particular point, is always to be encouraged. About the general connection between Christianity and politics, our position is more delicate. Certainly we do not want men to allow their Christianity to flow over into their political life, for the establishment of anything like a really just society would be a major disaster. On the other hand we do want, and want very much, to make men treat Christianity as a means; preferably, of course as a means to their own advancement, but, failing that, as a means to anything–even to social justice.[5]

Lewis' sarcastic prose illumines the complacency of Christians regarding politics and social justice. The Christian faith is not centered on receiving but giving to others who are in need. The deceptiveness of Satan has dulled the senses of many Christians to involve themselves in the arena of politics and social justice in an effort to improve lives and society.

The great revivalist, Jonathan Edwards, stated it best in the mid 1700s as he made this insightful comment; "Satan's most effective device was that while believers were fending off open opposition in front of them "the devil comes behind 'em, and gives a fatal stab unseen."[6] Like Moses comments in Numbers 32:23, Edward's statement was true not only in his own era but also today. Citizens are exposed to many visible barrages from various sources; however, they fail to notice the more subtle attacks that are being waged against our lineage. Unfortunately, the financial impact is the least damaging of the three major areas related to child maltreatment.

Societal Impact

One of the most ironic dynamics of child abuse and neglect is the effect that it has on the attitudes of people within societies worldwide. Given the level of financial devastation inflicted upon children and adults (reflected by the financial data in Figures 4-1 and 4-2), a natural assumption would be that there would be an overwhelming amount of support from the tax-paying citizens toward those who work directly with children and their families. It would seem that these employees would be highly valued both publicly and financially because of the work that they perform. However, in most instances public support is absent and it is replaced by public criticism of these professionals and their efforts on the front lines of the battle.

Many times employees of protective services are victims of patronizing remarks for a variety of reasons. In some cases, employees of children's services are immediately associated with the problem, and underappreciated as a result of that association. This lack of appreciation occurs not only toward the staff of children's services but also toward many others who provide public services. For example, after the terrorist attacks that occurred on September 11, 2001, and the natural disaster of hurricane Katrina in

August 2005, the fireman and policeman who demonstrated great courage and strength received appreciation for only a brief period before the country continued with business as usual. The process of desensitization was discussed earlier. The lack of appreciation for those who provide public services is related to the perception that adequate resources, training, and knowledge are available to those employed by state and federal agencies. Those who work feverishly to combat social ills and natural disasters deserve better from those they seek to protect. Frequently however, they lack support from state legislators and upper level management and also lack the resources to accomplish their duties.

What would happen if every social service agency was forced to close because each caseworker had resigned to seek a more lucrative job that was publicly appealing and appreciated? What would be the condition of our communities if this were to occur? There would be no one to investigate abuse and neglect allegations, develop effective treatment plans, or monitor high-risk situations for families in a state of crisis. How might our communities look if this were to happen?

Could it be that the criticism of public servants should be replaced with prayer, blessings, and support? We are instructed by the apostle Paul to pray for those who are in positions of authority. People tend to be critical of the efforts of caseworkers whenever they perform poorly, however most do not understand the complex dynamics involved in their line of work. Rarely are positive reports of appreciation shared with the public regarding the tremendous work that is accomplished daily by these men and women who are committed to engage the enemy. Countless numbers of lives are saved daily because of their efforts.

Employees of these agencies do need to be held accountable for the job that they do to ensure that every child and family is receiving appropriate services. However, it is a difficult task for a caseworker to manage a caseload of twenty families while at the same time the caseworker is attempting to maintain some semblance of normalcy for themselves and their families. Most are doing so with limited resources.

How did society develop this mindset? Where did the critical attitudes toward public servants who provide a safer environment originate? Recall the *indirect costs* of child maltreatment that were discussed earlier in this chapter (one of the categories was labeled *Adult Criminality*). *Prevent Child Abuse* reported "violent crimes in the U.S. costs $426 billion per year. According to the *National Institute of Justice*, 13% of all violence can be linked to earlier child maltreatment."[7] That's roughly $55 billion per year that's being spent on criminals who were traumatized by child maltreatment. The actual number of adult criminals who were abused or neglected as children and who are now serving time due to poor decisions, is staggering. Without the intervention of our public servants (e.g. caseworkers), how many more violent crimes would occur in our society? Which one of our family members would be the victim of burglary, rape, or even murder without the efforts of the employees of the local social service agency in our communities?

The lack of resources allocated to these agencies is another ironic dynamic of abuse and neglect. Caseloads for many social workers are enormously high. Management within these agencies understand that legislators have not allocated enough state and federal funds to hire enough full-time employees to reduce caseloads to manageable sizes. Employees question why elected officials fail to provide the necessary resources to effectively care for children of the parents who voted them into their political office. Could there possibly be some sort of deception by Satan that's clouding their judgment? Are their personal agendas and the agendas of their constituents who fund the political campaigns more important than the lives of the innocent?

Not only are most social service agencies lacking in human resources, but many lack the operational and financial resources (i.e., quality facilities, vehicles, technical support, training, etc.) needed by staff to accomplish their very important job functions. Many agencies are housed in antiquated shopping centers, and their employees are given substandard vehicles to transport the children for which they are providing services. Even more saddening is the fact that many agencies cannot afford luggage for the children that are taken into custody, and they transport children from one placement to another with their belongings being carried in garbage bags. What message is being sent to these beloved little children regarding their self-worth?

Jesus teaches in Matthew 25:45-46: "Assuredly, I say to you, inasmuch as you did not do it to one of the least of these, you did not do it to Me. And these will go away into everlasting punishment, but the righteous into eternal life." Caring for those who are perceived as "the least of these" within our communities (e.g., the homeless, prisoners, the sick and shut-in, widows, orphans, and even abused and neglected children) is high on Christ's list of priorities. Where are we as a society morally and ethically, and how did we arrive at this point? Denial, pride, indifference, casting blame onto others, and sins of omission provide a starting point. Members of society can no longer remain desensitized to the sin that has been accepted as the norm. No longer should citizens be expected to be satisfied with an expected percentage of loss of life. While we are impacted from both finance and society, attention must be focused on the most devastating area–the consequences of child maltreatment on individuals.

Impact On Individuals

Regardless of how profound the financial and societal impacts may be, they pale in comparison to the effects of child maltreatment upon children. The effects of child abuse and neglect can follow individuals into adulthood as they carry feelings of shame, guilt, and anger, because they have never had the opportunity to disclose the abuse or neglect they suffered as children. When individuals are called forward during church services to petition the Lord for relief from past abuse (physical, emotional, sexual, or neglect), scores of adults flood the altars for prayer concerning the pain that has been hidden deep within.

Case Study: While visiting a high management group home I had the privilege of interviewing one of the young men who had been placed there for approximately two months. During the interview it became apparent that he had become hardened by the *system* and was not remotely interested in anything but *aging* out of the system and getting away from everything that reminded him of family or the state where he was placed. It was discovered during the interview that the young man was sixteen-years-old and had been in the custody of the state since he was nine years of age. What was even more shocking was that the group home where he now stayed was his thirty-second placement since he came into care. He did not exhibit any faith in society's willingness to care for him. All he desired to do was to *make it* to his eighteenth birthday so that he could get away from what was considered to him as an oppressive system that did not care about him.

The following table lists both consequences and behaviors that children exhibit when they have been through painful abuse and neglectful experiences. No attempt will be made to categorize the behaviors relative to particular maltreatments. In many instances, children behave in similar ways regardless of the maltreatment. The purpose of the table is to provide insight into the possible conse-quences of child maltreatment on children. This information will help you see what children must learn to cope with as they carry hidden baggage from their past. In many instances they carry this to adulthood.

Figure 4-3

Impact of Abuse and Neglect Upon Individuals[8]

Death	Poor cognitive functioning
Brain damage	Agressive behavior
Subdural hematomas	Depression
Scarring	Post traumatic stress disorder
Long-term disability	Anxiety
Laxity of muscle tone around anus	Developmental problems
Thickening of skin folds around anus	Insecure attachment
Sexually transmitted diseases	Erosion of self-esteem
Pain in the genital area	Intergenerational transmission
Internal inflammation	Inappropriate sexual behavior
AIDS	Pregnancy
Poor health	Delinquency
A failure to thrive	Violence
Anemia	Runaway
Dental problems	Substance abuse
Developmental problems	Self destructive behavior
Psychological problems	Multiple alter egos
Stress	Criminal behavior
Extreme personalities	Unconscious transmission of abuse
Inappropriate guilt	Difficulty enjoying sexuality
Dissociation	Victim-perpetrator cycle
Changes in academic performance	Poor language comprehension
Low IQ scores	Loss of protection
Prostitution	Suicide
Behavioral withdrawal	Long-term neuroendocrine effects
Psychopathology	Interpersonal problems
Neurobiological effects	Peer relationship problems
Anger	

In no way are the contents of this table an exhaustive list of the possible results of abuse and/or neglect. Depending upon the severity of the abusive situation and the resiliency of the child, one might observe one or a combination of these behaviors in children who have been traumatized. Many of these symptoms do not surface until adulthood when an event or a progression of events triggers memories of an abusive or neglectful incident.

Children have retreated into multiple personalities in an effort to mentally disconnect from a traumatic incident. This development allows the child to mentally ease the pain associated with the incident for a period. Multiple personalities (or dissociative personalities) are difficult to treat and require the help of the LORD and the work of a qualified counselor to unravel the convoluted mental web that has been woven. Helping people understand how dysfunction occurs is vital to their recovery. This is addressed in the chapter on healing. The remainder of this chapter explores the spiritual effects of child maltreatment.

Spiritual Impact of Child Maltreatment On Individuals and Families

This study examined a biblical foundation for godly parenting in chapter 3. A further examination of the harmful influence of the world, the flesh, and the devil offers a better understanding of the importance of godly parenting and the potentially devastating consequences of the absence of godly nurturing.

When child maltreatment occurs the individual is harmed on several different levels. One of those areas is that of the soul. Tony Evans writes, "a lot of Christians get nervous when someone mentions psychology. But psychology is simply a study of the soul. It comes from the Greek word *psyche*, which means "soul." Your soul is made up of three parts: your intellect, the ability to think; your will, the ability to choose; and your emotions, the ability to feel. It's your personality."[9] When a parent or caregiver harms or allows a child to be harmed or neglected it can affect that manner in which that child thinks and feels. It can also distort that child's decision-making ability. We often see this manifested in what social workers call "acting-out" behavior.

A number of surveys have been taken to discover what entices women to pursue prostitution. These surveys have revealed that the majority of them were sexually abused as children. Sexual abuse distorted these women's ability to reason and lowered their self-worth. In essence, they began making poor decisions because of the effect that the abuse had upon their soul. We saw similar effects in the case studies in chapter two of Henry Lee Lucas, Pee Wee Gaskins, and Charles Manson. Their "souls" were impacted in such a manner that lives were destroyed, families were devastated, and communities were gripped with fear as a result of their poor decisions. Unlike these distorted souls, Ellen, mentioned in chapter 1, was able to allow the healing process to develop. She allowed her soul to be renewed and refreshed by following the LORD's plan for spiritual healing from the pain of her past.

[1] *The Preacher's Complete Homiletic Commentary: The Fourth Book of Moses, Called Numbers,* (Grand Rapids, MI, Baker Books, 2001), 559.
[2] Ibid., 559–560.
[3] Source: *Prevent Child Abuse America.*
[4] Source: *Prevent Child Abuse America.*
[5] C. S. Lewis, *The Screwtape Letters,* (New York, NY, Simon & Schuster, 1961), 87.
[6] George M. Marsden, *Jonathan Edwards: A Life,* (New Haven & London, Yale University, 2003), 285.
[7] Suzette Fromm, [http://64.233.161.104/search?q=cache:Uqs8L9Q11QwJ:www.preventchildabuse.org/learn_more/research_docs/cost_analysis], referenced 8 September 2006.
[8] South Carolina Department of Social Services, *Human Services Training Manual,* 2003.
[9] Tony Evans, *Free at Last: Experiencing True Freedom Through Your Identity In Christ* pp. 21-22

DRYING SILENT TEARS

Chapter Five
The Perpetrators of Abuse and Neglect

*Therefore give to Your servant an understanding heart to judge
Your people, that I may discern between good and evil. For who
is able to judge this great people of Yours?*

1 Kings 3:9

As King David lay on his death bed, he gave specific instructions to Nathan, the prophet, and Zadok, the priest, to anoint his son.
The next king of Israel would be Solomon. Adonijah, the son of
Haggith, tried to circumvent the authority of King David by pro-
claiming himself as king. Later, Adonijah was executed for his
deceit. Zadok then took the horn of oil and poured it onto Solomon's
head, anointing him king. Early in King Solomon's reign, the LORD
visited him in a dream as he slept in the land of Gibeon. He specifically asked Solomon in 1 Kings 3:5, "Ask! What shall I give you?"
Solomon responded to God with a profound prayer. Solomon
requested that the LORD "give to Your servant an understanding
heart to judge Your people, that I may discern between good and
evil. For who is able to judge this great people of Yours?"

Solomon's prayer for understanding (wisdom) and discernment
was a phenomenal request that catapulted him into a realm of divine
favor and standing with the LORD. To serve as an effective leader of
God's people would require wisdom that many fail to obtain.

According to Mordechai Cogan, "Moses also was not up to the task of judging Israel because of their number (so in the Deuteronomic depiction of the institution of judges in Deuteronomy 1:9-12); it is the fulfillment of YHWH's promise to the patriarchs (e.g. Genesis 15:5; 28:14) that has brought about this difficulty."[1] A special gift provided by the LORD would enable the king to effectively lead God's people in righteousness. Cogan later refers to the heart in tune to the LORD as "a heart that listens and considers. Skinner translated: "a discerning mind" as the heart being the organ of comprehension in ancient Hebrew physiology."[2]

Solomon demonstrated the foresight of a seasoned commander in asking for God's guidance to have an understanding heart. Volkmar Fritz provides further insight into the listening heart stating, "according to the biblical understanding, the heart is not the place of feelings but the center of understanding and will. The heart determines the spiritual direction of a person, which is also the place through which God influences and determines the human person."[3] The key for a successful reign as king of Israel would rest in Solomon's heart. As Israel's king, Solomon did not desire to be merely a *judge* like most ancient monarchs who operated in a docile manner, but rather sought after a penetrating discernment to effectively rule God's people.[4] "The prayer for a 'listening heart' is not simply that he should be made clever or discerning, but that he be attuned to Yahweh's guidance and purpose for justice. Thus the new king wants to have the sensitivity and wisdom to order Israel's life by the will of Yahweh."[5]

The second part of Solomon's request was that he be able to "*discern between good and evil.*" In essence, Solomon did not want to rely solely upon human intellect, but wanted divine guidance and intervention from the LORD in determining what was good and bad in society. Fritz writes, "the ability to distinguish between good and bad is not only a necessary prerequisite to reach a verdict but also a basic qualification to lead a proper life. Good is what is in accordance with law and morality because only then is a peaceful existence possible. Bad is the opposite of good; the disturbance of the unity of the ethos of the clan and thus of society as a whole."[6] King Solomon knew deep within his soul what many of his predecessors failed to understand. He needed the help of the LORD in order to make quality decisions regarding other people.

The LORD was extremely pleased with Solomon's prayer as He responds in 1 Kings 3:11-13:

> Then God said to him: "Because you have asked this thing, and have not asked long life for yourself, nor have asked riches for yourself, nor have asked the life of your enemies, but have asked for yourself understanding to discern justice, behold, I have done according to your words; see, I have given you a wise and understanding heart, so that there has not been anyone like you before you, nor shall any like you arise after you. And I have also given you what you have not asked: both riches and honor, so that there shall not be anyone like you among the kings all your days."

1 Kings 3:11-13

Solomon was blessed by God to rule with wisdom and discernment for a season. As noted in earlier chapters, he failed to follow all of the commands of the LORD, which resulted in the sacrificial death of his own child. However, his prayer for wisdom and discernment serves as a model for Christians as they seek to understand the nature and profile of perpetrators of child abuse and neglect.

The wisdom of the LORD guides a person in determining how to cultivate a safe environment for children. As Solomon understood early in his reign, it took God-given wisdom to discern between good and evil and to help His people. With the help of the LORD, the knowledge obtained by professionals in the field of children's services can be used to broaden the knowledge base of those who desire to protect the LORD's children.

There is no exact method of determining a specific representation or profile of a perpetrator of any of the four maltreatments (sexual abuse, physical abuse, physical neglect, mental injury). The *Child Abuse Sourcebook* reveals that "there is no single known cause of child maltreatment. Nor is there any single description that captures all families in which children are victims of abuse and neglect. Child maltreatment occurs across socioeconomic, religious, cultural, racial, and ethnic groups. While no specific causes definitively have been identified that lead a parent or other caregiver to abuse or neglect a child, research has recognized a number of risk factors or attributes commonly associated with maltreatment."[7] Perpetrators of child maltreatment come from every background, ethnicity, gender, and social class represented in the human race. However, there are categories that have been recognized which assist in defining behavioral patterns of the maltreatments and provide a better understanding of the characteristics of the perpetrators of child maltreatment.

Perpetrators of Sexual Abuse

Much of the information gathered regarding those who abuse and neglect children centers on the profile of those who sexually molest children. There are certain typologies or definitions that will help distinguish between someone who *may pose a potential threat* of harm and *one who actually sexually abuses children*. In many instances the terms *child molester* and *pedophile* have been used synonymously in describing child sexual abusers. According to former FBI supervisory special agent Kenneth Lanning,

> ...not all pedophiles are child molesters. A child molester is an individual who sexually molests children. A pedophile might have a sexual preference for children and fantasize about having

112

sex with them, but if he does not act on that preference or those fantasies, he is not a child molester…some pedophiles might act out their fantasies in legal ways by simply talking to or watching children and later masturbating…some might have sex with dolls and mannequins that resemble children…others may act out child fantasy games with adult prostitutes."[8]

It is necessary to distinguish between the two as we seek to accurately identify potential threats of harm to children and those who have actually sexually molested children.

There are also myths regarding sexual predators that need to be dispelled in order to unmask the enemy and discover the truth about their nature.

The myth that the typical child molester as the dirty old man in the wrinkled raincoat has been reevaluated based on what we have learned about the kinds of people who sexually victimize children. The fact is child molesters can look like anyone else and even be someone that we know and like. The other part of this myth, however, is still with us, and it is far less likely to be discussed. It is the myth of the typical child victim as a completely innocent young girl walking down the street minding her own business. It may be more important to confront this part of the myth than the part about the evil offender especially when addressing the sexual exploitation of children and acquaintance child molesters. Child victims can be boys as well as girls, and older as well as younger. Not all child victims are "little angels." They are, however, human beings.[9]

Satan has deceived many people with these myths that are accepted as reality. Child molesters and pedophiles operate under the radar of public opinion. The following chart provides more detail regarding the myths related to sexual predators that target children.

Figure 5-1
Myths of Child Molestation[10]

Myth:	The child molester is a "dirty old man."
TRUTH:	The majority of child abusers are under the age of 35.

Myth:	The offender is a stranger to the child.
TRUTH:	In almost three out of four cases, the offender and the victim know each other.

Myth:	The child molester is retarded.
TRUTH:	There are no significant differences in intelligence between incarcerated child molesters and the general public.

Myth:	The child molester is an alcoholic or drug addict.
TRUTH:	Drug abuse is essentially not a concern; almost one in three reported themselves as having an alcoholic problem.

Myth:	The child molester is a sexually frustrated person.
TRUTH:	Many child abusers are married, and many others have sexual outlets with other people.

Myth:	The child abuser is insane.
TRUTH:	Few child molesters are mentally ill or legally insane.

Myth:	Children are more at risk from gays.
TRUTH:	No studies show gays abuse children more than heterosexuals.

Though the listing of myths provided in Figure 5-1 is not exhaustive, it does provide insight into the misperceptions that many in society have regarding child molesters. The following behavioral descriptors of child molesters provide assistance in uncovering the deceptiveness of the devil and offer a framework in understanding the characteristics of sexual predators.

Patterns & Behaviors of Child Sexual Molesters

Both law enforcement officials and human service professionals categorize sexual predators as either situational or preferential child molesters. Whether an individual is considered a situational or preferential child molester is not as important as the fact that each poses a threat to the welfare of children. The following explanation of these categories distinguishes between the two types of molesters.

Figure 5-2
Situational Molesters[11]

	Regressed	Morally Indiscrimiate	Sexually Indiscriminate	Inadequate
Basic Characteristics	Poor coping Skills	User of people	Sexual experimention	Social misfit
Motivation	Substitution	Why not?	Boredom	Insecurity and curiosity
Victim Criteria	Availability	Vulnerability and opportunity	New and different	Non-threatening
Method of Operation	Coercion	Lure, force, or manipulation	Involve in existing activity	Exploits size, advantage
Pornography Collection	Possible	Sado-masochistic detective magazines	High likely: varied	Likely

Situational Molesters do not have an innate desire to sexually molest children. Due to a variety of reasons or situations, however, they may engage in sexually molesting a child. According to Lanning, "For such a child molester, sex with children may range from a 'once-in-a-lifetime' act to a long-term pattern of behavior. The more long-term the pattern, the further down the continuum he may move. He will exhibit more and more of the behavior patterns of the preferential-type offender. The situational-type molester usually has few child victims."[12] The fact that situational offenders do not have a compulsive desire to molest children does not make them any less dangerous than preferential offenders, just different.

Professionals who have gathered data on sexual predators characterized as situational molesters have discovered *four distinctive patterns of behavior* that this type of offenders tends to follow. The first behavior noted is that of the regressed offender. The *regressed* offender typically uses a child as a substitute for a preferred sexual partner. This type of offender has poor coping skills, and his victims are usually chosen based upon availability. "His principal method of operation is to coerce the child into having sex. This type of situational child molester may or may not collect child or adult pornography. If he does have child pornography it will usually be the 'best kind' from an investigative point of view–homemade photographs or videos of the child that he is molesting."[13]

The second type of situational offender is the *morally indiscriminate* offender. This type of offender has a lifestyle of abuse, which may include abuse of spouses, co-workers, friends, or children. There are typically limited boundaries with this type of individual because they are morally bankrupt and will lie, cheat, perform acts of theft, and engage in any other form of morally corrupt behavior. "His primary victim criteria are vulnerability and opportunity. He has the urge, a child is available, and so he acts."[14] This type of offender is violent in nature and collects magazines and other materials that are violent in nature.

Sexually indiscriminate offenders are similar to *morally indiscriminate* offenders in that they do not value humans and that they do not discriminate in their abuse. This type of offender becomes bored with sexual routines and embraces sexual experimentation. They seek new and different sexual liaisons and collect a variety of sexually explicit material.

The last type of situational offender is the *inadequate offender*. The *inadequate offender* "is difficult to precisely define and

116

includes those suffering from psychoses, eccentric personality disorders, mental retardation, and senility. In layperson's terms he is the social misfit, the withdrawn, the unusual. He might be the shy teenager who has no friends of his own age or eccentric loner who still lives with his parents."[15] The *inadequate offender* takes advantage of children and the elderly because of a size advantage. They are insecure and act on built-up impulses that can involve instances of sexual torture.

Although *situational molesters* do not actively seek to molest minors, they nonetheless are a threat to God's children and need to be identified and reported to law enforcement officials.

Figure 5-3
Preferential Molesters[16]

	Seduction	Introverted	Sadistic
Common Characteristics	1.Sexual preference for children 2. Collects child pornography or erotica		
Motivation	Identification	Fear of communication	Need to inflict pain
Victim Criteria	Age & gender preferences	Strangers or very young	Age & gender preferences
Method of Operation	Seduction process	Non-verbal sexual contact	Lure or force

"Preferential-type child molesters have definite sexual inclinations. For many that preference includes children, and they are the ones it would be most appropriate to refer to as pedophiles."[17] As we have discovered, not all pedophiles act on their fantasies and become child molesters. Pedophiles have been defined as "an adult who is sexually attracted to a child or children."[18] The *preferential molester* who focuses on children (pedophile) has sexual fantasies and erotic thoughts of either male or female minors. The *preferential molester* can be best described via the following behavioral characteristics.

Seductive preferential offenders lure children into compromising situations using such tactics as offering gifts, providing them with attention, offering affection, and grooming them over a period of time. They can exhibit an inordinate amount of patience until "victims arrive at a point where they are willing to trade 'sex' for the attention, affection, and other benefits they receive from the offender."[19] The grooming process of these child molesters can take the form of games or other forms of seemingly normal behavior. Law enforcement profiles reveal that many of the seductive preferential offenders have abused multiple victims that "may include a group of children in the same class at school, scout troop, or neighborhood...His adult status and authority are also an important part of the seduction process."[20] This type of molester does not have difficulty accessing children. The offender's main problem is effectively disengaging from the molesting relationships built up over a period of time after the children become too old.

The *introverted preferential* child molester does not necessarily have the relational or communication skills needed to seduce children. This individual fits the stereotype of how many members of society view child molesters. The introverted molester will tend to visit places where they have access to children (parks, playgrounds, children's events, etc.). They typically have very poor communication skills or have a fear of communicating with potential victims. These offenders normally target very young children or strangers. Lanning states,

He may expose himself to children or make obscene telephone calls to children. He may utilize the services of a child prostitute, or travel to a foreign country, or use the internet to communicate with children. Unable to figure out any other way to gain access to a child, he might even marry a woman and have his own children, very likely molesting them from the time they are infants.[21]

The behavioral patterns of *introverted* molesters are predictable due to their personality and inability to groom or seduce children.

Lastly, the *sadistic* preferential child molester is one of the most harmful of all sexual predators. Sadistic molesters are aroused as they cause a tremendous amount of harm to their victims. "This pattern of behavior characterizes the offender whose sexual preferences predominately include the need to inflict psychological or physical pain or suffering on his victims in order to be aroused or gratified."[22] *Sadistic* molesters are the most dangerous type of child molester according to law enforcement officials. It has been reported that "he is more likely than any other preferential-type child molesters to abduct and even murder his victims.[23] The pain that is inflicted upon children is so traumatic that they find it difficult to communicate to others the harm that has been done. In an effort to prevent prosecution, *sadistic* molesters will murder their victims and dispose of them in a manner that prevents detection.

The aforementioned types of child molesters provide a paradigm for the various types of dysfunctional behaviors exhibited by those who sexually abuse children. Additionally, there have been numerous pedophile organizations established whose aim is the sexual abuse of children. "The *Rene Guyon Society* is named after a former judge in Thailand and author of several books and papers dealing with human sexuality, including that of children. It was formed in 1962 by seven couples during a lecture on human sexuality, and it has grown into a national association of people who are vitally interested in promoting legislation that would permit adults to have sex with children."[24] Another organization established during the 1970's is The *North American Man/Boy Love Association*. According to Stephen T. Holmes and Ronald M. Holmes, "The *North American Man/Boy Love Association* (NAMBLA) was founded in 1978 in part as a response to the gay movement in Boston at the time. However, we should note here that most homosexuals are as opposed to the NAMBLA as heterosexuals are. This pedophile organization has several goals: (a) evangelizing the nature of the relationship between adult males and young boys, (b) educating the general public about the benefits of child sex, and (c) freeing all those who engage in sex with children from oppression and criminal prosecution."[25]

Other organizations established to sexually harm children include The *Childhood Sensuality Circle* (formed in 1971), the *Pedophile Information Exchange* (PIE), which was formed in England in 1974, and The *Howard Nichols Society*, which was formed in 1981. The founder, David Sonenschein, published material related to molesting children. "In one pamphlet published by the Society, Sonenschein provided hints for child molesters when selecting victims: 'Friends are a good source...It's also a good idea to get to know the parents...You can get babysitting tasks.' He goes further into details about the best way to sexually abuse children."[26]

Female Sexual Molesters

To this point the discussions of sexual abuse has centered on the male perpetrator. Rarely does the subject of female perpetrators of sexual abuse take place. Julia Hilsop reports that the notion of female sexual offenders is "incongruent with societal notions of femininity...(as) societal silence on this topic has allowed women who are molesting children to remain hidden. It is only recently that the existence of female sexual abusers has been occasionally considered by individuals who are not victims."[27] It is rare indeed that female molesters gain the same amount of attention as do their male counterparts.

Data gathered by the *U.S. Department of Health and Human Services* reveals that in the year 2000 there were 1,659 cases of sexual abuse indicated with the female parent acting alone, 3,276 cases indicated with the female parent participating in sexual abuse along with another person, and 3,409 cases involving both parents.[28] These statistics do not include the data collected on residential facility staff, other relatives, foster parents, or child daycare providers. Nor do they include those cases that were never reported due to the fallacy that females do not sexually abuse children.

Unfortunately there has not been a significant amount of research on the female sexual child molester. Most of the information regarding the behavioral patterns of sexual molesters is based upon male perpetrators. According to Hislop, "females may not fit the profiles and patterns of male offenders. Preliminary evidence is mounting to suggest that female sex offenders may differ from males in important ways, including patterns of offenses, psychological histories, motivations for offenses and treatment needs."[29] Most professionals are not trained in the area of female sexual molesters, which hinders child victims from being able to fully disclose molestation that has taken place. "Campbell and Carlson found that even among those highly trained in the area of sexual abuse treatment, few were trained on the topic of female sexual abusers. They surveyed over 1400 conference attendees who had worked with child sexual abuse victims or offenders for an average of 7.7 years, with a yearly average of 62 clients. Fewer than 40% of those working with female offenders had been trained in the area."[30]

With the lack of training and public complacency regarding female offenders, many have been allowed to harm children without having to face the consequences for their behavior.

The following provides a limited profile of background information compiled on female sex offenders:

1. Commonly found in histories of female offenders are backgrounds that include severe trauma.
2. Studies reveal that the vast majority of them have been sexually abused in childhood.
3. Some case studies have revealed incestuous relationships.
4. Some have been raped in adulthood.
5. Reports from studies reveal that some have been physically abused as children.
6. Family pathology studies reveal incestuous relationships with siblings in which poor parental relationships were present and/or unstable home environments were found.
7. A variety of psychological problems are commonly found in female perpetrators, although not all female sex offenders meet diagnostic criteria for a psychiatric diagnosis.
8. Psychological disorders, violent behavior, and other forms of dysfunctional behavior have been noted in many case studies of female offenders.[31]

Although there is much to learn regarding the profile of female sexual predators, people must be diligent in their pursuit of justice for the innocent children in our communities. The blinders that have veiled the eyes of many in society relative to female sexual offenders need to be removed. Strategic efforts must be pursued to enhance the safety of all children, allowing them to thrive in a nurturing environment.

Satan will go to unimaginable lengths as the primary perpetrator of sexual abuse. The Christian community must arm themselves with the necessary resources (i.e., knowledge, understanding, discernment, strategies, etc.) and diligence to effectively combat the tactics of the devil. He continues to tempt men, women, and juveniles alike to sexually harm children.

Patterns and Behaviors of Emotional Abusers

In chapter 2 the emotional abuse of children was defined as a repeated pattern of caregiver behavior or extreme incident(s) that convey to children that they are worthless, flawed, unloved, unwanted, endangered, or only of value in meeting another's needs. The perpetrators of emotional abuse verbally denigrate children in such a manner that it causes lasting damage to their emotions and their sense of self-worth. To briefly recap the behaviors exhibited by the perpetrators of emotional abuse the following list of behaviors constitute this form of child maltreatment:

1. Spurning (belittling, degrading, shaming, or ridiculing a child; singling out a child to criticize or punish; and humiliating a child in public
2. Terrorizing
3. Exploiting or corrupting that encourages a child to develop inappropriate behaviors
4. Denying emotional responsiveness
5. Rejecting
6. Isolating
7. Unreliable or inconsistent parenting
8. Neglecting mental health, medical, and educational needs
9. Allowing child to witness intimate partner violence[32]

The emotional abuse of children is usually caused by the inability of parents to appropriately communicate with their children. There are certain behavioral patterns exhibited by perpetrators of this form of abuse that will assist in identifying potential threats of harm to minors.

Parental attributes in cases reported of psychological maltreatment (Emotional Abuse) include poor parenting skills, substance abuse, depression, suicide attempts or other psychological problems, low self-esteem, poor social skills, authoritative parenting style, lack of empathy, social stress, domestic violence, and family dysfunction. A number of studies have demonstrated that maternal affective disorder and/or substance abuse highly correlate to parent-child interactions that are verbally aggressive.[33]

The children who are at risk of emotional abuse can be found in many of the following dysfunctional parental circumstances:

1. Children of parents involved in contentious divorces
2. Children who are unwanted or unplanned
3. Children of parents who are unskilled or inexperienced in parenting
4. Children whose parents engage in substance abuse, animal abuse, or domestic violence
5. Children who are socially isolated or intellectually or emotionally handicapped

Perpetrators of emotional abuse are difficult to detect due to the nature of the offense. However, the LORD is able to give wisdom, understanding, and discernment (as He did with Solomon) to help those who desire to help protect His children and those who may not understand the harm that they are causing through their verbal berating behavior.

Patterns and Behaviors of Physical Abuse

Arguably the most harmful form of child abuse is physical abuse. The evidence provided by the *U.S. Department of Health and Human Services* shows that approximately 1,586 children were killed in the year 2007 due to physical abuse.[34] The statistics gathered by this agency reveal a fairly consistent pattern regarding the annual number of fatalities and injuries to children. Several variables are related to the behavioral patterns of perpetrators of physical abuse. Experts in the field of child maltreatment have recently come to a consensus that there are an interrelated number of perpetrator characteristics that are involved in physical abuse. According to Cynthia Crosson-Tower, this level of consensus has not always been the case, as she states, "Early in the 1970's, 1980's, and 1990's a variety of models evolved that might be loosely categorized into the following categories: the psychodynamic or character-trait models...the interactional models...and the environmental, sociological, culturally based models."[35] The following will provide insight into situations and behavioral patterns that experts have noted are associated with physical abuse.

1. Environmental/Life Stress Variable–Poverty (in some instances), lack of finances, multiple relocations, unsupportive neighborhoods, and an ineffective support system increase the level of stress in the lives of parents.

2. Social/Cultural/Economic Variable–Child rearing practices differ significantly across cultures to the degree that what some may consider abuse, others may not. The economic climate puts families under a great deal of stress. The climate of violence may also be channeled into violence within the family.

3. Risk Assessment and Physical Abuse–There may be child risk factors (younger children are more vulnerable, children whom parents see as difficult, children who have not bonded adequately), parental risk factors (depression, personality disorders, serious "life problems", domestic violence, lack of problem-solving abilities), and family system risk factors (isolated families, poor relationships with extended family and others within the community, strained relationships

within the family, unemployment, illness, estrange-
ment).[36]

Not all families that may be experiencing portions of the aforementioned variables or those considered to be a part of high risk categories are potentially abusive families. These areas merely represent the patterns and behaviors that have been documented by children's service professionals regarding those who have physically
abused children.

Patterns and Behaviors of Neglectful Parents

The data from the *U.S. Department of Health and Human
Services* reflects that in the year 2007 an astonishing number of
children were neglected: 436,944.[37] The cases of neglect represent
over one half of the total number of cases of child maltreatment
indicated during that year. As with the other maltreatments, it has
been discovered that neglectful parents follow certain patterns of
behavior that have been documented by investigators. This information can be helpful for those seeking to prevent children from being
harmed. Please note the behavioral patterns of neglectful parents
and caretakers.

1. Neglectful parents are seemingly indifferent to their
   children, disciplining them more out of their own
   need for quiet or convenience than out of a concern
   for what the child is learning.
2. They exhibit a poor capacity to solve problems or set
   goals for the future.
3. Because of their own inadequate childhoods, negative experiences with school, and unsatisfying adult
   relationships, they are ill-equipped to instill hope in
   their children, encourage them in school, or model
   for them the roles that society expects of functioning
   adults.

4. Neglectful parents are less involved with others, less able to control impulses, less verbally accessible, and less equipped with pride in their accomplishments or workmanship.

5. These parents may lack knowledge in the areas of attending to their children's needs, housekeeping and cooking skills, nutrition, child development, medical care, and the need to set limits for children.

6. They may also lack motivation in the form of energy to attend to their children or feel that they are the best judge of what is best for their children.

7. Polansky, Borgman, and DeSaix (1972) describe these parents as having infantile personalities.

8. Some neglectful parents/caretakers can be described as apathetic-futile as they seem to have given up on living.

9. Others are described as being impulse-ridden as they exhibit a low frustration tolerance, little ability to delay gratification, and extremely poor judgment.

10. Other neglectful parents may be: mentally retarded, reactive-depressive, or psychotic.[38]

A pattern of behavior that was not linked to physical neglect, but can be linked to other child maltreatments, is the dynamic of substance abuse by parents, caretakers, or perpetrators. When drugs or alcohol are ingested, they impair the ability to properly function in making mature, appropriate decisions. It is reported,

> Abuse of alcohol or drugs is often present in cases of child neglect. Child Protective Services (CPS) agencies indicate that substance abuse is a factor in a growing percentage of child neglect cases. Estimates range from a low of less than 24 percent to 80 to 90 percent of all child maltreatment reports…earlier studies found that 52 percent of the children removed from their homes for severe child abuse or neglect had at least one parent with a history of alcoholism.[39]

As with the patterns of behavior associated with other forms of child maltreatment, not all parents who exhibit these behaviors or have these tendencies abuse or neglect their children. However, those cases of abuse and neglect that have been investigated reveal that the perpetrators tend to display many of the characteristics that have been mentioned. Seemingly insurmountable odds are stacked against us in effectively combating this sin. However, under the leadership of the Holy Spirit, wisdom can be given to the Christian community to strategically determine how an effective partnership can be formed with those agencies whose mission it is to provide safety for children.

---

[1] Mordechai Cogan, *The Anchor Bible: 1 Kings,* (New York, Doubleday, 2000), 187.

[2] Ibid., 187.

[3] Volkmar Fritz, *1 and 2 Kings: A Continental Commentary*, (Minneapolis, MN, Fortress, 2003), 38.

[4] H. D. M. Spence, *The Pulpit Commentary*, (Grand Rapids, MI, Eerdman's, 1950), 52.

[5] Walter Brueggemann, *Smyth & Helwys Bible Commentary: 1 & 2 Kings*, (Macon, GA., Smyth & Helwys, 2000), 47-48.

[6] Volkmar Fritz, *1 & 2 Kings*, 39.

[7] Dawn D. Matthews, *Child Abuse Sourcebook*, (Detroit, MI, Omnigraphics, Inc., 2004), 243.

[8] Kenneth V. Lanning, *Child Molesters: A Behavioral Analysis*, (National Center for Missing & Exploited Children, 2001), 19.

[9] Ibid., 3.

[10] Stephen T. Holmes & Ronald M. Holmes, *Sex Crimes: Patterns and Behaviors*, (Thousand Oaks, CA, Sage Publications, 2002), 95.

[11] Frances P. Reddington and Betsy W. Kreisel, *Sexual Assault: The Victims, the Perpetrators, and the Criminal Justice System*, (Durham, NC, Carolina Academic, 2005), 223.

[12] Kenneth V. Lanning, *Child Molesters: A Behavioral Analysis*, 25.

[13] Ibid., 25.

[14] Ibid., 26.

[15] Ibid., 26.

[16] Reddington and Kreisel, *Sexual Assault*, 223.

[17] Kenneth V. Lanning, *Child Molesters: A Behavioral Analysis*, 27.

[18] *The American Heritage Dictionary of the English Language*, Houghton Mifflin, 2003, [http://www.thefreedictionary.com/pedophile], referenced 30 October 2006.

[19] Kenneth V. Lanning, Child Molesters: A Behavioral Analysis, 27.

[20] Ibid., 27.

[21] Ibid., 28.

[22] Ibid., 28.

[23] Ibid., 28.

[24] Stephen T. Holmes and Ronald M. Holmes, *Sex Crimes: Patterns and Behaviors*, 108.

[25] Ibid., 109.

[26] Ibid, 110-111.

[27] Hilsop, Julia, *Female Sex Offenders: What Therapists, Law Enforcement and Child Protective Services Need to Know*, (Ravensdale, WA, Issues Press, 2001), 29.

[28] *Child Maltreatment 2000*, 52.

[29] Hislop, Julia, *Female Sex Offenders*, 47.

[30] Ibid., 48.

[31] Ibid, 101-145.

[32] Steven W. Kairys and Charles F. Johnson, *The Psychological Maltreatment of Children-Technical Report*, (Pediatrics, Vol. 109, No. 4, April 2002, [http://www.pediatrics.org/cgi/content/full/109/4/e68], referenced 1 November 2006, 1.

[33] Ibid., 4.

[34] U.S. Department of Health and Human Services, *Child Maltreatment 2000*, 53.

[35] Cynthia Crosson-Tower, *Understanding Child Abuse and Neglect*, (Boston, MA, Pearson Education, 2005), 97.

[36] Ibid., 99-102.

[37] Jill Goldman and Marsha Salus, *A Coordinated Response to Child Abuse and Neglect*, 24.

[38] Cynthia Crosson-Tower, *Understanding Child Abuse and Neglect*, 80-87.

[39] Matthews, Dawn D., *Child Abuse Sourcebook*, (Omnigraphics Inc., 2004), 260.

Chapter Six
Places of Rest

"Now when they had departed, behold, an angel of the LORD appeared to Joseph in a dream, saying, "Arise, take the young Child and His mother, flee to Egypt..."

Matthew 2:13

We discovered in chapter 3 that the LORD desires for children to be cared for in safe environments or *places of rest*. James Hatch described these *places of rest* as havens where children dwell without fear of being harmed.

The gospel according to Matthew describes the diligence and care of how the LORD preserved human life through the provision of resting places for His children. Deceptive acts by King Herod were devised to harm the baby Jesus. Herod first summoned the wise men privately,

Then Herod, when he had secretly called the wise men, determined from them what time the star appeared. And he sent them to Bethlehem and said, "Go and search carefully for the young Child, and when you have found Him, bring back word to me, that I may come and worship Him also."

Matthew 2:7-8

Then, an angel of the LORD appeared to Joseph with an urgent plea to move his family from their current location to a place where they would be out of harm's way (Matthew 2:13).

The deceptive patterns of many perpetrators of abuse and neglect mirror Herod's behavior. Those who intentionally seek to harm children tend to base their behavior on deceit. Herod's sole intent was to murder the baby Jesus. He called a secret meeting with the wise men to discover the exact location of the baby Jesus. Like any addict looking to fulfill the pleasures of the flesh, perpetrators of abuse and neglect seek to gain access to those whom they want to harm through the use of various tactics. They will use any method necessary to gain access to those upon whom they prey. Like Herod, perpetrators will tell untruths in order to gain the favor of those who can give them a clear path to what they desire, which is to bring harm to God's children.

Matthew 2:12 reveals that the LORD delights in revealing the strategies of the adversary. When the wise men came to the house and worshiped the infant Christ, they were warned by the LORD not to return to Herod for he would surely bring harm to them for not following through with his request. Heeding the warning of the LORD instead, the wise men returned to their homeland using a different route. This infuriated Herod and revealed his true motive for wanting to know the whereabouts of the Infant.

Biblical records reveal that one of the most heinous acts in the history of mankind took place after Herod found out that he had been tricked. Herod became enraged and,

> sent forth and put to death all the male children who were in Bethlehem and in all its districts, from two years old and under, according to the time which he had determined from the wise men. Then was fulfilled what was spoken by Jeremiah the prophet, saying: "A voice was heard in Ramah, Lamentation, weeping, and great mourning, Rachel weeping for her children, refusing to be comforted, because they are no more."
>
> Matthew 2:16-18

Herod ordered that all male children under the age of two be murdered in an attempt to kill the Christ child. Historical records document that the slaughter of these innocent children only added to the list of hideous crimes committed by Herod. Historians note that,

> He put to death several of his own children and some of his wives whom he thought were plotting against him. Emperor Augustus reportedly said it was better to be Herod's sow than his son, for his sow had a better chance of surviving in a Jewish community.[1]

In spite of Herod's efforts, the angel of the LORD provided Joseph and Mary with the wisdom to seek a *place of rest* for the Infant.

Knowledge gained through years of experience in the field of human services has revealed to child services experts, several practical steps for the care of children to minimize the possibility of child maltreatment. There are no structures, systems, or methodologies that are without flaws. However, practical steps exist that can reduce the possibility of children being placed in harm's way and provide the God-given right to dwell in *places of rest*.

Steps for a Safe Household

Parenthood is filled with memorable moments that make the journey of raising children rewarding. From the first glance in the delivery room to observing that person blossom into an adult, parents are given the gift of raising God's children to the best of their ability. These moments are often captured through the use of photography and videos as parents and caregivers develop a lifetime of memories which are passed from one generation to the next. In an effort to assist in maintaining restful safe havens, 1 Kings 3:18-19 illustrates how the best intentions of parents can lead to tragedy.

Then it happened, the third day after I had given birth, that this woman also gave birth. And we were together; no one was with us in the house, except the two of us in the house. And this woman's son died in the night, because she lay on him.

The passage reveals a tragedy that is often overlooked. Most often this passage is used to describe the process of how King Solomon would reveal whose child remained alive. The other lesson is that the child described in this passage became the victim of an unfortunate, yet not so rare, tragedy. This parent sought to comfort and console the infant by placing him in her bed to rest. Scripture provides evidence that the infant either died from suffocation or trauma as a result of the mother laying on the child.

Child fatality review committees in our states review many of these instances on a regular basis thousands of years after this biblical occurrence. These are some of the findings that members of these committees have shared.

- Infants are allowed to sleep with adults, other children, or even pets. As the adults, children, and pets roll over in their sleep infants cannot move and are trapped under a body, a limb, heavy bedding (i.e., sheets, comforters, etc.), or trapped against a wall. In the first 9 months of 2008, 64 children under the age of two have died due to unsafe sleeping conditions in the state of South Carolina alone.
- Many of those who have died in these unsafe sleeping conditions have been placed on their stomachs.
- Some adults have placed children on their chests while lying on a couch. While on the chests of their caregivers, infants have rolled between the adult and couch resulting in suffocation.

- In an effort to quiet infants, parents and caregivers prop bottles in the child's mouth. This practice has led to suffocation if the child gets too much milk or can't breathe while feeding.
- Adults have placed children in unsafe/unacceptable places in order to contain them–tupperware containers, baby car seats (for sleeping), on a sofa (alone), on beds or pillows surrounded by soft bedclothes, in bassinets using adult pillows as a mattress.

Children should be placed only in approved cribs, bassinets, or infant beds. Other places may be convenient or even part of family tradition, however, are they safe? The following excerpts from *The Complete Guide to Making Your Home Safe* by Heberle and Scutella further emphasize the need for careful attention to be paid in establishing safe havens.

Crib Safety
- If you assemble a crib yourself, make sure all the nuts and bolts are firmly secured so they can't be loosened by someone's fingertips; then periodically check them.
- Test the crib by raising and lowering the side rails before putting into service.
- Push, pull and shake the crib by its end panels and sides to see how strong the construction is.
- All of the crib's slats and posts should be solidly attached and space no more than two and three-eighths apart from one another.
- A crib mattress should fit snugly. If you can fit the width of two of you "average size" fingers between the mattress and sides, the mattress is too small or

the crib is too large. A baby could slip into the gap and suffocate.

- Mattress support hooks should stay firmly in their brackets when the mattress is maneuvered or jostled about.
- The top rail of a lowered drop side should be at least nine inches above the mattress support at its lowest setting, so an infant can't fall out.
- Avoid a crib with a drop side that can be released too easily or that can be opened with only a single motion for each lock.
- All cribs should have bumper pads around the entire crib interior, attached by snaps and no less than six straps.
- Fancy decorations that can come off and break apart are not safe.
- Corner posts or "finials" that protrude above the tops of the end panels can snag garments and strangle a baby.[2]

Heberle and Scutella provide other valuable practical tips regarding the selection and use of high chairs, walkers, changing tables, toy chests, and even toys. The reoccurring theme in their study reveals that parents and caregivers should conduct thorough examinations on a regular basis of the areas where children are cared for. This ensures that the possibility of a child being harmed is not due to negligence.

Sitters and Child Care Facilities

Nothing raises the level of anxiety in a parent more than leaving their child with a babysitter or in a child care facility for the first time. Making the appropriate choice of caregiver is extremely important. The well-being of children depends upon making appropriate choices relative to their caregivers.

Although babysitters are not required to have any form of state licensing, they should be thoroughly investigated just as any licensed day care facility would examine potiental staff.

When considering sitters, Debra Holtzman suggests the following:

- Ask around or hire an agency. Draw on recommendations from friends, relatives, neighbors, clerics, or local organizations.
- Consider age. The sitter should be at least 13 years of age...with a good starting age for babysitting around 15 or 16.
- Conduct interviews including the following (evaluating the candidates attributes, know how they will handle discipline, see how they interact with the children.
- Check references
- Investigate the candidates background
- Find out about the candidate's health
- Ask about the candidate's training
- If the candidate will be transporting your child, check the driving record
- Set guidelines
- Give the sitter a tour of your home
- Point out the do nots of activities of your child
- Explain what is expected of the sitter
- Devise an emergency plan
- Be concise with parting instructions
- Be observant while you are at home, check up during and after your absence[3]

Holtzman is just as adamant about the selection of day care facilities. She suggests that child safety be at the top of the lists of priorities for these environments. Holtzman provides the following advice for parents who seek safe child care facilities for their children.

- Investigate the licensing of the centers on your list
- Focus on location (choosing a place close to the route between home and work for at least one parent)
- Find out how long each center has been in business (older establishments are more likely to be stable and provide a broad range of references)
- What do other parents say about the centers on your list
- Find out about employees and the ratio of children to caregivers
- Find out about hiring practices
- Ask questions about holidays, schedule flexibility, and fines
- Look at programs and policies
- Learn what the centers expect from parents
- Observe the day care center (Is it safe? Is it clean? Are toys and equipment age-appropriate and in good condition? Do the caregivers and children appear happy? Do they seem healthy? Are there separate cribs for each child?)
- Check references
- Pay attention to your child[4]

Parents should not operate in fear or paranoia, but should carefully examine the settings where they leave their children.

Strangers Lurking

There is a common phrase used by parents when their children reach the age to be out of their reach: "Never talk to strangers." This is considered *THE RULE* when children leave the home and we assume that if *THE RULE* is obeyed, our children will be safe from evil. Talk show host, Oprah Winfrey, who is a staunch supporter of the rights of children aired a show in 1993 that provided insight which illustrated how well *THE RULE* works with children. The show titled *Child Lures* provided shocking evidence as to how children can easily be lured away from safe havens in a suburban park. Gavin De Becker writes,

> Oprah's producers and I [Ken Wooden] approached several young mothers in a suburban park to ask for their cooperation with our experiment. Each mother emphatically insisted that her child would never leave the park with a stranger, then watched in horror from a distance as her youngster cheerfully followed me out of the park to look for my puppy. On average, it took thirty-five seconds to lure each child away from the safety of the park.[5]

In a matter of 35 seconds, the lives of families could have been changed forever with the assumption that *THE RULE* works. In actuality it does not work as children are lured into harms way more often than we would like to believe as predators lure them away from safe environments with enticing words, toys, or other things that are attractive to children. To totally rely upon a child to guard them against these evil ponds of the adversary is irresponsible. That is why it is imperative that everyone be aware of what is going on around them and take responsibility for all citizens, even if they are not a part of our responsibility. De Becker provides the following list of websites that provide aides for parents to help prevent the experiment that Oprah conducted in becoming a tragic reality.

- *Child Lures*–a comprehensive plan for prevention & awareness of the lures used by perpetrators to harm children: **www.childlures.org**
- *Alanon*–assists families dealing with alcoholism and addiction: **www.al-anon.alateen.org**
- *Civitas Initiative*–a nonprofit organization whose mission it is to provide parents, professionals, and policymakers with better ways to protect, educate, nurture, and enrich children: **www.civitas.org**
- *Yello Dino*–dedicated to preventing the abduction and abuse of children through the use of unique con-fidence-building programs. It is a musically based program that helps children remember vital personal safety information. **www.yellodyno.com**[6]

By implementing the very practical steps provided by each of the organizations mentioned above, we as a society can reduce the number of child abductions and the pain that is caused in families that lose children in this manner.

A Treasure Chest of Knowledge

The National Center for Missing and Exploited Children is one of the best and most underutilized resources in the fight against child maltreatment. The organization has a wealth of informational tools readily available for parents, communities, and organizations that can assist in educating each of us on how to prevent child maltreatment. One of the more interesting and revealing sources of information provided by the organization is the statistical analysis of online victimization. The factual information provided in the following table is startling, given the amount of time that our children and youth spend online each day. The report is based upon a study done with a representative sample of 1,501 youth between the ages of 10-17 who are frequent users of the Internet.

- Approximately one in five received sexual solicitation or approach over the Internet in the last year.
- One in thirty-three received an aggressive sexual solicitation–a solicitor who asked to meet them somewhere; called them on the telephone; sent them regular mail, money, or gifts.
- One in four had an unwanted exposure to pictures of naked people or people having sex in the last year.
- One in seventeen was threatened or harassed.
- Approximately one quarter of young people who reported these incidents were distressed by them.
- Less than 10% of sexual solicitations and only 3% of unwanted exposure episodes were reported to authorities such as a law enforcement agency, an Internet Service Provider, or a hotline.
- About one quarter of the youth who encountered a sexual solicitation or approach told a parent. Almost 40% of those reporting an unwanted exposure to sexual material told a parent.
- Only 17% of youth and approximately 10% of parents could name a specific authority, such as the *Federal Bureau of Investigation, Cyber Tipline*, or an *Internet Service Provider*, to which they could make a report, although more said they had "heard of" such places.
- In households with home Internet access, one third

of parents said they had filtering or blocking soft-
ware on their computer at the time they were inter-
viewed.[6]

With the frequency of attempts to lure minors into compromising situations the need for more community involvement is more
apparent each day. It is impossible to perceive that a single entity
can conquer these social problems. It is also irresponsible on the
part of every person in our society to not take part in the efforts to
keep our future generations safe. There are *General Parental Tips*
provided by the Center that further equip parents to provide safe
havens. The following is a summation of those tips.

1. Make sure you know where each of your children are at all
times.
2. Never leave children unattended in an automobile, whether
it is running or not.
3. Be involved in your children's activities.
4. Listen to your children.
5. Take the time to talk to your children.
6. Teach your children that they have the right to say NO.
7. Be sensitive to any changes in your children's behavior or
attitude.
8. Be sure to screen babysitters and caregivers.
9. Practice basic safely skills with your children.
10. Remember that there is no substitute for your attention and
supervision.

This is just a sample of available information provided by the
National Center for Missing & Exploited Children. They have personal safety guides for children, Netsmartz workshops which assist

in Internet education, and a host of other resources that help make our communities safe. What the center does not have is the community support needed to activate the necessary strategies required to create resting places for our children. This is where each citizen in our society makes the decision to be a part of the solution or be onlookers, as in the case study of Kitty Genovese that we examined earlier.

What decision will you make? How do you choose to respond to the challenge of caring for those who are not able to protect themselves. The last chapter of this book provides various ways in which each of us can partner in creating safe environments. As in the case of Joseph and Mary, the LORD is giving each of us the discernment needed to combat the evils of child abuse and neglect. It is a privilege to partake in such a venture. Look at the blessing that came out of the obedience of Joseph who heeded the warning and moved Christ to a safe place. Our eternal salvation rested on his decision to obey the LORD. Lives may lie in the balance of our decisions. Let us take to heart the information provided in the last chapter as we seek to provide places of rest for all children.

---

[1] Dallas Seminary Faculty, *The Bible Knowledge Commentary* (Wheaton, Il., Victor Books, 1983), 21.

[2] David Heberle & Richard Scutella, *The Complete Guide To Making Your Home Safe*, (Cincinnati, OH, Betterway Books, 1995), 37-40.

[3] Debra Smiley Holtzman, *The Safe Baby: A Do-It-Yourself Guide to Home Safety*, (Boulder, CO, Sentient Publications, 2005), 159-165.

[4] Ibid, 165-170.

[5] Gavin De Becker, *Protecting the Gift: Keeping Children and Teenagers Safe*, (New York, NY, Random House Publishers, 1999), 80.

[6] David Finkelhor, Kimberly J. Mitchell, and Janis Wolak. *Online Victimization: A Report on the Nation's Youth*, (Alexandria, Virginia, National Center for Missing & Exploited Children), ix.

Chapter Seven
An Unearthly Healing

But when the multitudes knew it, they followed Him; and He
received them and spoke to them about the kingdom of God, and
healed those who had need of healing.

Luke 9:11

An integral part of Christ's earthly ministry was that of healing those who were sick, afflicted, and troubled. It was through these acts of healing that the power of Christ and the supernatural dynamics of the kingdom were visibly demonstrated. Those who were healed became living testimonies of the greatness of the Savior and His loving compassion. Though Christ's ministry was multifaceted, His healing ministry impacted everything else He did. Healing the afflicted caused many to believe in His name. Nothing showed the supernatural power of the LORD any more than when He restored a person's physical health.

In the ninth chapter of Luke's gospel the LORD empowered His disciples with authority over all demons and gave them the ability to heal diseases. Coupled with this empowerment, Christ commanded the disciples to proclaim the kingdom of God. Scripture discloses in Luke 9:6 that the disciples were obedient to the LORD's commands: "So they departed and went through the towns, preaching the gospel and healing everywhere." Although Christ empowered the disciples to minister the gift of healing, He continued to heal those that were in need whenever and wherever the Heavenly Father guided Him–"Most assuredly, I say to you, the Son can do nothing of Himself, but what He sees the Father do; for whatever He does, the Son also does in like manner" (John 5:17). Scripture declares that when the disciples returned from ministering to others, they returned to Christ and gave an update of what they had achieved:

> And the apostles, when they had returned, told Him all that they had done. Then He took them and went aside privately into a deserted place belonging to the city called Bethsaida. But when the multitudes knew it, they followed Him; and He received them and spoke to them about the kingdom of God, and healed those who had need of healing.

> Luke 9:10-11

The LORD was concerned not only with the spiritual needs of people but also with their physical needs. His compassionate nature transcends time as He continues to heal those that are wounded. Without question, the highest priority of Jesus Christ is the salvation of lost souls. It is the Father's desire that humanity be reconciled unto Himself through faith in His Son, Jesus Christ. God's desire is also to care for those in need of healing. As it was with the disciples, the body of Christ has been empowered with the authority to heal the sick and broken-hearted. Christians are the avenue through which Christ desires to serve as a conduit of healing and through which the kingdom of God is proclaimed. The incarnate Christ is no longer visibly present as He was with the disciples. The Holy Spirit is ever present today to empower believers to proclaim God's Word and empower Christians to be vessels of mercy who administer healing.

The book of James (5:14-16) provides evidence of the Christian's role in healing. James calls for the elders of the church to pray the prayer of faith over those that are sick (who are to confess their sins) so that the LORD may heal those who are afflicted. The LORD is as concerned today as He was during His earthly ministry about those who are harboring pain internally and are in need of healing. He desires to comfort those who are afflicted today, just as He did during His earthly ministry.

Other scriptural accounts of Christ's healing ministry are found in Matthew and Mark:

> Then His fame went throughout all Syria; and they brought to Him all sick people who were afflicted with various diseases and torments, and those who were demon-possessed, epileptics, and paralytics; and He healed them.
>
> Matthew 4:24

> And they cast out many demons, and anointed with oil many who were sick, and healed them.
>
> Mark 6:13

Christ and his disciples were compassionate and genuinely concerned with healing those in need of care. The disciples understood that they had no power of their own to heal others but were chosen vessels used by Christ to administer healing through prayer. Just as electrical current must have a conduit to distribute the powerful current, so were the disciples of Christ used as conduits of Christ's healing in the New Testament.

The LORD wants to continue to heal those who are hurting today. As seen in previous chapters, the pain caused by abuse and neglect can leave indelible scars on individuals. Those scars can be cleansed by the Holy Spirit and the Word of God. The conduits in which healing will be administered in the twenty-first century are not the original disciples but members of the global Christian community. These Christians, who make themselves available to be used by the Holy Spirit, are channels through which healing is administered to the hurting.

Healing

Ruveni and Speck offer the following definition of healing:

> One definition of healing is to overcome, to restore to original integrity, to return to a sound state. Family members in an emotional crisis experience the strife, the hurt, the isolation, and lack of strength to cope with their dysfunctional relationships and life pressures. Such family members need indeed to be able to increase their ability to cope, to overcome, to restore their strength, to change–to heal.[1]

Though the text was published over twenty years ago, it encompasses secular therapeutic philosophy regarding healing. From a Christian perspective, however, this definition misses the mark in three crucial areas. First, there is no mention of the work of the Holy Spirit, in the healing process. Second, it does not include the Word of God, which provides the matrix for healing. Last, the definition assumes that returning to a "sound state" is returning to a place of wholeness.

> Another methodology used in secular counseling is that of psychotherapy. Therapists agree that defining psychotherapy is difficult and encompasses a comprehensive array of processes. It is best described by comparing it with counseling. "Essentially, counseling stresses the giving of information, advice, and orders by someone considered to be an expert in a particular area of human behavior, while psychotherapy is a process of helping people discover why they think, feel, and act in unsatisfactory ways. A counselor is primarily a teacher, while a psychotherapist is essentially a detective."[2]

Each of these methodologies assists clients in discovering the source of unwanted behavior, thoughts, or dysfunctions in their lives. However, just as the aforementioned definition of healing was incomplete without the presence of the Holy Spirit and God's Word, the use of psychotherapy or secular counseling is temporal and fails to address the LORD's role in the restoration process.

The following statement regarding psychotherapy illustrates the absence of God in the process. "The basic theory of person centered therapy is that if the therapist is successful in conveying genuineness, unconditional positive regard, and empathy, then the client will respond with constructive changes in personality organization."[3] Person centered therapy helps individuals sort out the issues in their lives. However, without minimizing the usefulness of secular counseling methods, there is a missing element that will leave an eternal void; namely, the LORD.

There are numerous approaches to helping people work through difficult situations in their lives. Various psychoanalytical, humanistic, behavioral, cognitive, and social-learning approaches seek to modify unwanted behavior and reshape individuals in a manner that is considered normal by the standards of the society in which they live.[4] As with the other methods of therapeutic interventions, the responsibility for successful outcomes lies solely with the therapist and the client, without intervention from LORD. As valid as these approaches are to healing, none can reach their maximum potential without the inclusion of God Himself (in the Person of the Holy Spirit) and His Word.

Our study of the fall of man in Genesis 3 illustrates the beginning of the chaotic spiritual nature of man relative to his fallen nature. This sinful state is compounded by the influences of the world. The Holy Spirit and the Word of God not only serve as the primary means of healing but also as the foundational elements through which healing occurs. In 1 Corinthians 2:5 this point is made clear by the apostle Paul as he writes, "...that your faith should not be in the wisdom of men but in the power of God." Reliance upon the Holy Spirit and principles found in God's Word is paramount in the process of effective, lasting healing. An emphasis on biblical principles does not negate the efforts of secular therapists but enhances their efforts. The wisdom of non-Christian psychologists, psychiatrists, and other secular therapists without the reliance upon the Holy Spirit and Scripture does not allow for complete healing to occur.

God's Word and the work of the Holy Spirit are crucial in restoring the wounded. In an effort to engage in complete restoration the issue of eternity has to be addressed. The non-believer who has been abused or neglected is still in a state of total depravity. Christ addressed the crowds in Luke 9 in the same manner in which He instructed His disciples. He not only healed the sick but proclaimed the kingdom of God. A more complete form of healing from abuse and neglect is gained through counseling, the work of the Holy Spirit, principles from God's Word, and a personal relationship with Christ. This reflects the biblical model demonstrated by Jesus as He ministered to both the spiritual and physical needs of those He encountered.

A more effective way of overcoming child maltreatment can be accomplished by members of the Christian community partnering with children's service agencies and secular therapists. Providing biblical principles needed to ensure that both emotional and spiritual wounds are healed is the Christian mission. The Christian community must become actively involved in bringing resolution to the sin of child maltreatment. The data gathered by the *United States Department of Health and Human Services* demands that the body of Christ get involved in the fight against child maltreatment.

Christians can no longer be dormant and delegate sole responsibility to governmental agencies. There has to be a partnership with children's service agencies to provide opportunities for complete healing.

Since the development of child welfare agencies, many children have not had the opportunity to experience complete restoration simply because that has not been the focus of these agencies. Individuals continue to harbor the pain, guilt, and shame associated with child maltreatment. In Matthew 16:19 the LORD proclaims, "And I will give you the keys of the kingdom of heaven, and whatever you bind on earth will be bound in heaven, and whatever you loose on earth will be loosed in heaven." Satan's attempts to keep people in bondage will be overcome by Christ's Kingdom. Christ gave believers the keys to the kingdom. Not only do they have access to the King, but they have the ability to introduce others to Him as well. According to Craig Bloomberg:

> Jesus promises Peter the "keys to the kingdom," apparently to be interpreted as the authority to "bind" and "loose." The metaphor of binding and loosing was variously employed in ancient Judaism but often was used for the interpretation of the Torah and for decision making more generally...But this translation reflects a fairly late, rabbinic usage; more immediate parallels suggest that one should pursue the imagery of keys that close and open, lock and unlock (based on Isaiah 22:22) and take the binding and loosing as referring to Christians' making entrance to God's kingdom available or unavailable to people through their witness, preaching, and ministry.[5]

A major component of the Christian faith is sharing access to the King with non-believers. Spreading the gospel of Jesus is the goal. As the gospel is shared, the King of kings provides eternal healing to those who embrace Him. God restores and redeems today just as He did through His original disciples.

The Complexities of Abuse & Neglect

In chapter 2 the subject of physical indicators and behavioral dynamics relating to abuse and neglect was introduced. Upon examination, it was noted that there are numerous negative behavioral traits associated with each of the four maltreatments (physical abuse, physical neglect, sexual abuse, and mental injury). Healing becomes more complicated when children are subjected to multiple maltreatments. A myriad of dysfunctional personality disorders can result if a child suffers from multiple traumatic events.

Those who have an opportunity to work with children harmed by perpetrators of child maltreatment understand that each child responds differently to trauma, depending upon several factors: coping skills, the nature and severity of the abuse and/or neglect, their level of resilience, and the care that they receive. The child's behavior may be categorized by one of the following four descriptions: (1) denying that the abuse or neglect ever occurred; (2) repressing the trauma as they place the painful memories within the recesses of their mind; (3) exhibiting dysfunctional behavior (oppositional defiant disorders, self-mutilation, promiscuity, suicidal ideations, etc.); (4) not adequately processing the trauma.

The *American Psychiatric Association* describes behaviors associated with traumatic events in the *Diagnostic and Statistical Manual of Mental Disorders* (DSM-IV) under the title of *Posttraumatic Stress Disorders*. The APA describes this disorder as follows:

> The essential feature of Posttraumatic Stress Disorder is the development of characteristic symptoms following exposure to an extreme traumatic stressor involving direct personal experience of an event that involves actual or threatened death or serious injury, or other threat to one's physical integrity; or witnessing an event that involves death, injury, or a threat to the physical integrity of another person, or learning about unexpected or

violent death, serious harm, or threat of death or injury experience by a family member or other close associate. The person's response to the event must involve intense *fear*, *helplessness*, or *horror*. The characteristic symptoms resulting from the exposure to the extreme trauma include *persistent re-experiencing* of the traumatic event, *persistent avoidance of stimuli associated with the trauma* and *numbing of general responsiveness*, and *persistent symptoms of increased arousal*.[6] [emphasis added]

Each of these dysfunctional behaviors can potentially hinder the development of healthy personalities, and they become an obstacle that children have to overcome if they are to experience complete wholeness.

Further evidence of this is given by Bessel Van Der Kolks, as he writes, "It should be noted that babies cannot control negative feelings that are larger than their capacity for joy. *This also shows why the single-largest effect of childhood trauma is the inability to control emotions throughout the rest of life*"[7] [emphasis added]. Without the ability to control one's emotions, living the victorious Christian life is challenging at best. Job describes this state of mental unrest in Job 3:26 as he laments, "I am not at ease, nor am I quiet; I have no rest, for trouble comes." It is not the nature of humans to naturally gravitate toward one of the aspects of the fruit of the Spirit–longsuffering–as described in the Bible. Humans attempt to alleviate pain by denial or by abusing medication. The lamentations of Job speak for many who suffer and cry out for relief from the pain that they experience daily. Before relief can be found, those who suffer must recognize that there is indeed an internal pain. The first stage of healing is facing the proclivity of denial.

Denial

The initial stage in the healing process is making a decision to be healed. For many people this is not an easy task to accomplish. A child inflicted with child maltreatment may experience and exhibit at least one, if not several, of the behavioral stages associated with grief and loss (denial, anger and guilt, despair and depression, acceptance). One of the elements of the *Grief and Loss* cycle that is commonly observed in those that have been traumatized is denial. Denial is simply "a refusal to acknowledge the truth…"[8] Most who are in denial behave in a manner that masks the pain hidden beneath the surface of their emotional threshold. The reason they are in denial is their inability to cope with the truth of what has happened in their lives. Several behaviors are associated with denial:

- Simple denial
- Minimizing
- Rationalization
- Intellectualizing or generalizing
- Blaming
- Diversion
- Bargaining
- Passivity
- Hostility[9]

Those in denial appear to behave in ways that are irrational to others who know the truth about the circumstances of their lives. The person in denial may attempt to avoid or behave in a defensive manner toward those who seek to help them work through the issues. Those in denial appear to live in a fantasy world. A willingness to work through the crisis situation is not even an option to them at this stage.

Denial can be viewed as a defense mechanism that promotes false hope and security. It is built on a fragile emotional foundation that can easily be toppled by a reoccurring offense or by recalling past child maltreatment. A number of unhealthy behavioral outcomes can surface as a result of being in denial. One of the most damaging is poor decision-making abilities. Typically these develop during a prolonged period of unresolved issues. These emotional flaws are evident in various facets of the lives of those in denial, and can become more frequent as time passes.

Other negative behavioral tendencies include the following: becoming socially isolated from others, projecting internal pain onto someone else in an effort to cope, improper rationalization of the abuse and/or neglect, thwarting efforts of others that may try to assist the person in working through the process of healing, and a continual development of a fantasy life in an attempt to project an aura of stability to those that are not aware of the traumatic event(s). One way to effectively counteract denial is to confront the situation that is hindering the fulfillment of a healthy lifestyle. Confronting pain is the beginning of living a life that is fruitful and honoring to the LORD. The crisis that served as a catalyst for denial must be confronted and adequately worked through so that fragile emotions are not being simply managed but completely healed. As this is accomplished, the life that was based upon false self-images begins to be transformed into what the LORD intended. Cecil Osborne speaks of this when he writes,

> Dishonesty is not limited to the overt theft or lies. A worse dishonesty consists in lying to ourselves, in denying our true feelings, in pretending that we feel one way when we really feel another, in a subtle refusal to face up to the kind of person we really are.[10]

The courage to confront the hurts of the past does not have to be accomplished alone. The LORD desires to help every individual confront and conquer the pain in their lives. It is also the will of the LORD that Christians assist those in need of healing by helping them confront their pain without judgmentalism. Through these joint efforts the wounds that lie beneath the surface can be confronted with the assistance of the LORD and His disciples.

Confronting Pain

Two passages that are frequently misinterpreted as they relate to healing from old wounds are 2 Corinthians 5:17 and Philippians 3:13-14. The misinterpretation has centered on the issue of the pain associated with traumatic events. Some have taught and preached in error, as they communicate that wounds which occurred before conversion to Christianity should die along with the old man and never be allowed to surface again with the new person in Christ. Unfortunately, this is not true. If memories and pain from past traumatic events have ever disappeared after conversion, it would certainly be the exception and not the rule. This faulty teaching damages the faith of new converts, because it could potentially cause doubt regarding their conversion experience. Coupled with doubting their conversion, some may experience guilt and potentially develop an even more skewed self-perception as they continue to feel pain associated with past child maltreatment. A careful examination of these passages reveals the intentions of the apostle Paul.

In 2 Corinthians 5:17, Paul writes to the church at Corinth about the commitment level of those who have believed in Christ as their Savior and LORD. The apostle shares the knowledge that he has gained as a maturing believer in Christ. He understands that when an individual accepts Jesus as Savior and LORD, they accept union with Him in his death and resurrection. Therefore, they commit to dying to self (the old creature) and pursuing the resurrected life (the new creature) of a new believer. The committed Christian no longer pursues youthful lusts but pursues Christ-likeness. Paul's use of the aorist tense in this passage implies that there is a definite break with the old lifestyle at conversion (old things passed away). There is a transition in tense from the aorist to the perfect tense in an effort to stress a continuous union with Christ as the result of pursuing the new things.[11]

156

An Unearthly Healing

In Philippians 3:13-14, Paul refers to the religious credentials he spoke of in an earlier portion of the chapter. He counts those things as "loss" which are described in verse 7, along with the achievements that he made under the guise of religious traditional practices as a member of the Pharisees. Paul refuses to rest on past laurels; as he is determined to continue his pursuit of the most prized accomplishment of all, which is having an intimate relationship with Christ. This is described in verse 10 as Paul is determined to "...know Him and the power of His resurrection, and the fellowship of His sufferings, being conformed to His death."

These passages indicate that there is new life after Christian conversion, but they do not indicate that the memories or the pain of the past will automatically vanish. On the contrary, the original language illustrates that there should be a continual pursuit of the new things pertaining to the Christian lifestyle. Scripture gives assurance to those who are born again that they now have direct access to the One who can provide healing from past memories that haunt them through the development of an intimate relationship with Christ.

Battling the Giants

Many events in the Bible illustrate the value of confrontation. Stories of godly confrontation are found throughout the Old Testament, such as the account of Moses confronting Pharaoh in Exodus 5-12 (as he requested that Israel be set free), and the story of Elijah confronting the prophets of Baal on Mount Carmel in 1 Kings 18 (the prophet had great confidence that no other gods would be able to defeat the LORD).

In the New Testament the benefits of godly confrontation are found in Acts 15: 36-41, as Paul and Barnabas engage in a heated exchange (v. 39). The result of this confrontation was the spreading of the gospel. Barnabas and Mark traveled to Cyprus, while Paul chose Silas and journeyed to Macedonia to share God's Word. Jesus Christ also had His share of confrontations during His earthly ministry. None was more prevalent than His confrontation and ensuing victory over Satan and death as He was crucified at Calvary, descended into Sheol to defeat death, and was raised from the dead on the third day. This confrontation has yielded phenomenal fruit, providing the opportunity for man (in his fallen state of depravity) to be reconciled to the LORD. None of this would have been possible without Christ confronting Satan and death at Golgotha.

Death by crucifixion causes excruciating pain to the physical body. According to Luke 22:42, Christ also suffered tremendous internal pain. In this passage Christ cries out to God the Father, "saying, 'Father, if it is Your will, take this cup away from Me; nevertheless not My will, but Yours, be done.'" Christ knew that he would be separated from God the Father, and it was that internal pain that caused Him to cry out from the cross, "*Eloi, Eloi, Lama Sabachthani* (My God, My God, Why Have You Forsaken Me)?" Even with the knowledge that He would have to experience internal pain that no human could imagine, Christ fulfilled His earthly ministry knowing that He would have to experience and confront pain.

Another biblical example provides a model for confronting areas that may appear insurmountable, but also provides an answer to some of the difficult questions of child maltreatment.

David: An Example of Godly Confrontation

An intriguing illustration of confronting seemingly insurmountable obstacles is found in 1 Samuel 17. David and Goliath's battle reveals how trusting in the LORD for guidance is of utmost importance when facing difficult situations. Trusting in the LORD builds the faith not only of the person who initiates confrontation, but also of those who may be in their vicinity when Godly confrontation happens.

Two armies were at a standstill fostering a confrontation between David and Goliath. Both armies were positioned to enter into battle but they were initially unwilling to engage each other in warfare. Scripture indicates in 1 Samuel 17:3 that the Philistines were positioned on one mountain while Israel positioned themselves across from them on another mountain. Between the two was the valley of Elah. The geographical implications revealed in surrounding passages imply that it was in the valley of Elah where the confrontation between David and Goliath occurred. Members of the Philistine army eventually initiated confrontation with the giant, Goliath. He was introduced as the intimidating force in the battle. According to scriptural evidence, Goliath stood at a height of six cubits and a span (estimates range between nine feet and eleven feet). This imposing figure continuously taunted and challenged the Israelites for forty days; yet, none of them accepted the challenge to come forward and confront this colossal enemy. The only one willing to confront the seemingly insurmountable giant was the youngest son of Jesse. David made the decision to step forward and assume the position of challenger.

David was baffled that no one would accept the challenge to go forward and confront the enemy of the LORD. Young David was not even a member of the Israelite army, but was responsible for tending his father's sheep in Bethlehem. How ironic that the LORD would use a young lad who was not considered a mighty warrior in the eyes of man to confront such a phenomenal, intimidating force such as Goliath. As the Philistines and Israelites postured, measuring themselves against one another, David arrived in time to witness Goliath once again challenging the Israelites.

Intimidation worked successfully for a number of days. Seeing that none of the Israelites would accept the challenge, David volunteered to face Goliath, much to the chagrin of his brothers. After convincing Saul to allow him to confront the giant, David was offered modern weapons. He refused the use of modern weaponry and chose his slingshot and five smooth stones. Scripture discloses that when confronted, the giant looked at David with disdain because of his age, stature, and appearance. David did not look the part of a mighty warrior but he understood he was not challenging the giant in his own power but "I come to you in the name of the LORD of hosts, the God of the armies of Israel, whom you have defied" (1 Sam. 17:45). With this knowledge David understood that he had the support of the "LORD of the hosts" (v. 45), which gave him a distinct advantage over the intimidating figure that held the Israelites at bay through psychological warfare. As a direct result of his faith, the LORD gave David victory over Goliath.

Biblical principles relative to this confrontation can be of great value to those hurt by child maltreatment. First, the people involved in this battle can be symbolically linked to trauma caused by abuse and neglect. The giant, Goliath, symbolically represents hidden wounds in the minds of those physically and/or emotionally wounded. These wounds can be both intimidating and colossal in the eyes of the wounded. They continue to haunt individuals daily, just as Goliath haunted the army of Israel. The pain can be so deeply entrenched into the cognitive processes of the wounded that they sometimes believe that complete victory and healing can never be achieved.

Second, the youthfulness of David represents those people who were wounded during their formative years. They may never be able to reach their full potential as productive adults. They become trapped inside a cauldron of victimization because of trauma from child maltreatment. Their lives are shaped by hopelessness, despair, anxiety, guilt, and shame, because they feel unable to confront the fears and lies that hold them captive. They have not been properly equipped to confront the enemy. David was verbally discouraged by his brother Eliab (v. 28) when he stepped forward to accept the challenge to battle Goliath. Eliab was embarrassed that this little shepherd boy, who had just been tending sheep, possessed more courage than all of the members of the army of Israel. From a human perspective, David was not qualified to pursue an encounter with Goliath. He was seemingly overmatched in every way; yet, David had faith in the LORD and knew that the battle was not his, but the LORD's. When faced with the decision of whether or not to confront those hidden wounds of the past, those who are wounded and have accepted Christ as their Savior and LORD need not dismay, but only recognize that the battle is the LORD's. Giving the battle to Him is an essential step to healing and victory.

The third biblical principle is related to the second. The disparity in size between David and Goliath gives the perception that David does not have a chance for victory. It was not David's physical stature that provoked the LORD to act on his behalf, but his measure of faith. David understood the principle found in 1 John 5:4 well before the apostle was inspired to write it. The passage states: "For whatever is born of God overcomes the world. And this is the victory that has overcome the world–our faith." Even though David did not know of Christ, since Jesus was not yet born, he knew of and believed in the God of Abraham, Isaac, and Jacob. David embraced the God who delivered the Israelites out of Egypt, who delivered Jericho into the hands of Joshua, and who had given him power to protect his flock from lions and bears with a simple slingshot and rocks. He would serve as a type of Christ in this confrontation as David, the good shepherd, who was willing to lay down his life in combat to protect the LORD's flock from an aggressive enemy.

Faith in the Spirit of the LORD is the primary weapon needed to confront the giant obstacles that have hindered healing in the lives of those that have been abused and neglected. Scripture declares in Zechariah 4:6, "'Not by might nor by power, but by My Spirit,' Says the LORD of hosts." Since the beginning stages of battle against Satan to this present time, the LORD has always been dependable to war against the enemy. It is a war that is to be engaged with divine power, not human effort. God has already won the war and desires for His children to depend on Him for victory in every battle. The LORD will go before His children and lead them through the healing process just as He led the children of Israel out of Egypt and into the Promised Land (see Exodus 14:21; Nehemiah 9:12; Psalm 78:14). He is a God of compassion that desires to heal the wounded. Gary Haugen writes:

> When it comes to the brutality of injustice in our fallen world, there is no place for an all-knowing God to hide–a God who "has compassion on all he has made" (Psalm 145:9). When the Israelites were oppressed in Egypt, God told Moses, "I have indeed seen the misery of my people in Egypt. I have heard them crying out because of their slave drivers, and I am concerned about their suffering" (Exodus 3:7). Today when the taskmaster beats the seven-year-old bonded child laborer in India for not rolling his quota of cigarettes, God sees and hears. When two police officers rape the runaway girl, he witnesses it. When mobs mercilessly hack to death thousands of Tutsi women and children, he suffers with them. Over and over in Scriptures God lets us know that he sees and hears the suffering of the oppressed. When the strong abuse their power to take from those who are weaker, the sovereign God of the universe is watching, and suffering.[12]

The compassionate, caring, and loving God will heal all who embrace Him through the Holy Spirit, the promises in His Word, and through His people who embrace the compassion that He has shown throughout the history of mankind.

Fourth, unlike Goliath, who boasted under the assumption that his size, strength, and experience would give him the victory, David advanced into the confrontation with a spirit of humility and dependence on the LORD–not in himself. If victory and healing are to occur, then the confrontation needs to be approached using godly rules of engagement. A spirit of humility and dependence upon the LORD are vital elements of godly confrontation. Scripture reveals in James 4:6, "God resists the proud, But gives grace to the humble." Through God's abundant grace, victory is secured by faith for those that humbly submit themselves to Him.

The last biblical principle is an act committed by David that reflects a principle also found in the life of Joseph. After David hurled the stone that became embedded in the forehead of Goliath, birth was given to a unique principle. In 1 Samuel 17 we read:

> Therefore David ran and stood over the Philistine, took his sword and drew it out of its sheath and killed him, and cut off his head with it. And when the Philistines saw that their champion was dead, they fled. Now the men of Israel and Judah arose and shouted, and pursued the Philistines as far as the entrance of the valley and to the gates of Ekron. And the wounded of the Philistines fell along the road to Shaaraim, even as far as Gath and Ekron. Then the children of Israel returned from chasing the Philistines, and they plundered their tents. And David took the head of the Philistine and brought it to Jerusalem, but he put his armor in his tent.

1 Samuel 17:51-54

The end results of this series of events is similar to what Joseph experienced in Genesis 37 when his brothers seized him and sold him to the Ishmaelites for twenty shekels of silver. Joseph was enslaved for a lengthy period of time, and was later falsely accused of sexual assault by the wife of Potiphar. The false accusations of the wife of Potiphar caused Joseph to spend more time in prison.

However, like David, Joseph was determined to confront his brothers in a spirit of godly confrontation. Human revenge was not Joseph's motivation. With God-given wisdom, Joseph turned a bad situation in his life into a blessing. This blessing protected his family and many others during the seven years of famine in Genesis 41-48. Genesis 50:20 reveals this principle clearly: "But as for you, you meant evil against me; but God meant it for good, in order to bring it about as it is this day, to save many people alive."

Satan meant evil against Joseph and against the army of Israel by utilizing imprisonment, false accusations, and intimidating forces (i.e., the person of Goliath). Yet, as Joseph and David humbly submitted to the LORD, Satan's attempts to hurt God's children were thwarted through godly confrontation. Just as the evil act of Joseph's brothers eventually led to the preservation of many lives during the period of famine, the act of David killing Goliath preserved the lives of many members of the Israelite army by using the evil that was meant to harm them for their good.

The Scripture indicates that David used the enemy's sword to decapitate the giant. He then took Goliath's head and brought it to Jerusalem as a testimony to the faithfulness of God by taking the enemy's main weapon (his sword) and turning it on him for good. The LORD can do the same for those who have been intimidated by the enemy through child maltreatment. The wounds attributed to abuse or neglect need to be confronted. The enemy has used emotional wounds to hold children and adults hostage as the result of psychological trauma they have experienced. The LORD can bring victory in these areas by His Word, by the power of His Holy Spirit, and through wise council and care from counselors and members of the Christian community. He will bring good out of evil. The evil may have been inflicted by a family member, as in the case of Joseph, or by a stranger like Goliath. Regardless of whom Satan used to bring harm, the LORD is still victorious and He wants all who have suffered abuse and neglect to be victorious. The enemy's attacks can then be used against him as the LORD heals those who have been abused and neglected. As healing occurs, powerful testimonies of the healing virtues of Christ help others to be healed and set free from the emotional bondage they endure. This parallels with what David accomplished by decapitating Goliath and marching through the streets of Jerusalem with the head of the giant as a testimony to the faithfulness of God. Scripture declares, "And they overcame him by the blood of the Lamb and by the word of their testimony, and they did not love their lives to the death" (Rev. 12:11).

Principles from God Meant It for Good

R.T. Kendall offers further insight on "God meant it for good" as he illustrates the manner in which the LORD is able to bring good out of evil. Kendall writes:

> Do we want to be used of God? Are we quite sure we are ready to be used of the LORD? God knows whether we are. In the case of Joseph, there was much sorting out in his personality that had to be done, and I can tell you this: God can do it. God, as He prepares us to do His work, will sort out our personality defects, many of which may have been superimposed upon us. It is easy for us to say, "I am like this because my mother was this way," or "My father did this or that." It is easy to blame our parents for the way we are. We may be shy. We may be forward. We may be reserved. We may be arrogant. But we should never think that any personality trait or hang-up (or any other blemish) rules us out as God's messengers to our generation, for God can deal with us. He certainly dealt with Joseph.[13]

Although he was not writing directly to those who have been abused or neglected, the principles shared by Kendall are relevant. In Kendall's text are a core group of truths regarding the life of

Joseph that will help make the decision to confront the hurts of the past much easier than trying to live with them or conquer them in isolation.

Figure 7-1
Spiritual Principles From the Life of Joseph
Source: R. T. Kendall

Spiritual Principle	Biblical Passage
1. God can transform those who have experienced difficulties into beautiful diamonds that can live the victorious Christian life and become a blessing to others.	"The God of all grace, who called you to His eternal glory in Christ, will Himself perfect, confirm, strengthen, and establish you." 1 Peter 5:10
2. When we are experiencing trying times in our lives we should know that it is for a reason, one of which could be to allow us to discover what is really in our hearts.	"…be ready in season and out of season…" 2 Timothy 4:2 • **in season**–times when we feel that God hears our prayers • **out of season**–times when we feel that God doesn't hear our prayers.
3. If we allow the LORD to lead us through trying times we can experience unspeakable joy.	"Weeping may last for the night, But a shout of joy comes in the morning." Psalm 30:5
4. As observed in Joseph's father, Jacob, self-pity can produce the following: • Sympathy for Self • Paranoia • Insensitivity to the feelings of others	"All these things are against me." Genesis 42:36
5. Strength is always found in the LORD and not in self.	"…Do not be grieved, for the joy of the LORD is your strength." Nehemiah 8:10"
6. Practice total forgiveness not primarily for the offender but more importantly for yourself.	"But Jesus was saying, "Father, forgive them; for they do not know what they are doing." Luke 23:34 [as He was being executed]

Principles one through five are not overwhelmingly difficult to practically apply to one's life. It is principle number six, the principle coined by Kendall as "Total Forgiveness," which gives some therapists and their clients problems.

Those who have endured suffering may ask:
- How can a loving and powerful God allow these evil things to happen to children?
- Why do bad things happen to good people?
- If there is a God, why does He not do something about these horrible people?

Some Christians who have not suffered from abuse or neglect may find it difficult to embrace the principle of suffering, especially as it relates to children. There are numerous Scriptures related to suffering but none more paramount than the words spoken to Timothy by the apostle Paul in 2 Timothy 2:12: "If we endure, we shall also reign with Him. If we deny Him, He also will deny us." Paul wanted to explain that the suffering endured on earth allows Christians the privilege of being identified with Christ in suffering and the assurance of reigning with Him for eternity.

Romans 8:18 reinforces this truth from Paul's perspective of suffering from internal circumstances: "For I consider that the sufferings of this present time are not worthy to be compared with the glory which shall be revealed in us." No one can minimize the pain, agony, and frustrations related to child maltreatment. From a human perspective, these are feelings that no one should ever have to endure. Sadly, man's blunder of sin in the garden, results in suffering caused by the evil nature of man.

Chitty provides an explanation for the mysteries surrounding suffering in a sermon from Psalm 131. This psalm was written by the same little shepherd boy, David, who confronted and killed the intimidating giant Goliath. In this passage David expresses childlike faith and trust in the LORD. In this Psalm, David had transitioned from a young person who achieved mighty exploits for the LORD to an adult whose sins against the LORD were well documented. Following Psalm 131 is the outline of the sermon titled: "Quickly Read, Slowly Learned." Charles Spurgeon said that this particular Psalm is read quickly, but having the ability to practically apply it to our lives is slowly learned.

Psalm 131

O LORD, my heart is not proud, nor my eyes haughty;
Nor do I involve myself in great matters,
Or in things too difficult for me.
Surely I have composed and quieted my soul;
Like a weaned child rests against his mother,
My soul is like a weaned child within me.
O Israel, hope in the LORD
From this time forth and forever.

Figure 7-2
Sermon Outline: Quickly Read, Slowly Learned

I. After a long life of success and fame, David has opted for humility. v. 1

II. In the midst of adversity, David adopted a toddler as his role model. v. 2

III. David has abandoned his quest for the understanding of all life's mysteries, and has opted instead for hope in the LORD. v. 3

  a. David told us in verse one that he had abandoned his quest for understanding the great mysteries of life. Man's reasoning will never bring contentment or peace.

b. Those who struggle with this tend to picture themselves as somehow intellectually superior to those who rest in the arms of the LORD.

c. May I submit to you the idea that life is not a struggle of intelligence vs. faith? Faith and intelligence are two sides of the same coin.

d. Faith is not the crutch of a weak mind. It is the human mind working as it was meant to work!

e. Faith is the human mind understanding three great truths…

> 1. Life as we know it is broken and marred by sin [i.e., abuse and neglect].

> 2. I am in no condition to judge what is "right" or "fair" in regard to Almighty God.

> 3. The only place I can find resolution in this present world is in the arms of Father God.

The mysteries of life are dealt with only in the arms of the Almighty, through prayer, His Word, and fellowship with His people.

The bad news to our human weakness is this:

God is unbending on this issue. He insists on sovereignty. King Nebuchadnezzar found out the hard way. "Now I praise and exalt and glorify the King of Heaven, because everything He does is right, and all his ways are just. And those who walk in pride He is able to humble."

The good news to our human weakness is this:

God's arms are wide open for each frightened, confused, and insecure little one to be held by Him, safe and secure, waiting for the day when God will set all things right, and all of life's mysteries will be made clearer and brighter than the noonday sun.

This sermon provides wisdom regarding life's mysteries related to suffering. The LORD offers assistance for all who suffer. True peace and contentment are found in His Word. Although God loves and cares for everyone, the world is riddled with sin and sinful people. As a result, people harm the innocent on a regular basis, including the vulnerable members of society, children.

In spite of the evil that is present, Christ's compassion for children is evident in Mark 10:

> Then they brought little children to Him, that He might touch them; but the disciples rebuked those who brought them. But when Jesus saw it, He was greatly displeased and said to them, "Let the little children come to Me, and do not forbid them; for of such is the kingdom of God. Assuredly, I say to you, whoever does not receive the kingdom of God as a little child will by no means enter it." And He took them up in His arms, laid His hands on them, and blessed them. [emphasis added]
>
> Mark 10:13-16

Is God Willing To Heal Me?

The emotional pain associated with traumatic abuse and neglect is overwhelming and can test the faith of those suffering. In many instances the hidden wounds result in unbalanced opinions of self-worth. These negative life experiences of abuse and neglect could potentially distort self-perception. They might even feel the LORD looks upon them negatively. They may even question whether the LORD is willing to heal someone like them.

These feelings and poor self-perceptions have to be processed through God's Word, so that the skewed self-perception is corrected biblically. Unfortunately, in social workers attempt to help restore distorted self-images, there is not a heavy reliance on God's Word. It is indicated throughout Scripture that God is a healer. It is this principle that the wounded need to embrace.

170

As sin, sickness, and pain entered into the world through sin, the LORD's mercy did not tarry. He proclaimed in Exodus 15:26:

> If you diligently heed the voice of the LORD your God and do what is right in His sight, give ear to His commandments and keep all His statutes, I will put none of the diseases on you which I have brought on the Egyptians. For *I am the* LORD *who heals you.* [emphasis added]

The original Hebrew language indicates that the LORD describes himself in this passage as *Yahweh Rapha*, which has been translated as *Jehovah Rapha*, or, the LORD as Healer. The root usage of the word *rapha* (healer) in the Old Testament has been documented as being related to healing both physical and spiritual wounds.[14] The process of restoration can be identified with righting something that is wrong, or healing someone that is sick or in a state of brokenness. Restoration is approached with the intent of transforming a state of brokenness into wholeness by the power of the Holy Spirit.

Theological evidence provided by Mike Flynn and Doug Gregg support this truth. While this is not an endorsement of the ministry of inner healing, Flynn and Gregg provide evidence of the compassionate, willing desire of Christ to heal his flock.

> In Jesus we see that God pursues our welfare. God's heart is moved for us. Jesus came to preach the gospel of the kingdom, to heal the sick and to cast out demons…The word that our Bibles translate "salvation" is most often used in the Gospels with reference to the healing of disease. Salvation is the activity of God directed toward those who suffer and are in need of his help.[15]

The LORD firmly established Himself as the true Healer of souls, although there were many counterfeits in the image of false gods that were vying for the loyalty of the children of Israel. Christ continued demonstrating the willingness to heal during his earthly ministry. The following is a list of passages related to Christ's earthly ministry of healing.

Figure 7-3

Spiritual Principle	Biblical Passage
Nobleman's son	John. 4:46
Demoniac in synagogue	Mark. 1:26; Luke 4:35
Peter's mother-in-law	Matt. 8:14; Mark. 1:31; Luke 4:38
Cleansing the leper	Matt. 8:3; Mark. 1:41; Luke 5:13
Paralytic	Matt. 9:2; Mark. 2:3; Luke 5:18
Invalid healed	John. 5:5
Shriveled hand	Mark 12:10;Mark. 3:1; Luke 6:6
Centurion's servant	Matt. 8:5; Luke 7:2
Raising widow's son	Luke 7:11
Demoniac	Matt. 12:22; Luke 11:14
Demoniacs of Gadara	Matt. 8:28; Mark. 5:1; Luke 8:26
Raising of Jarius' daughter	Matt. 9:18; Mark 5:42; Luke 8:41
Bleeding	Mt. 9:20;Mk. 5:25; Luke 8:43
Blind Men	Matt.9:27
Demoniac	Matt. 9:32
Daughter of Canaanite	Matt. 15:22; Mark 7:25
Deaf and dumb healed	Mark. 7:33
Blind man	Mark. 8:23
Afflicted child	Matt. 17:14; Mark. 9:26; Luke 9:37
Ten lepers	Luke 17:12
Blind man	John 9:1
Lazarus raised	John 11
Woman with spirit of infirmity	Luke 13:11
Man with dropsy	Luke 14:2
Blind men	Matt. 20:30; Mark 10:46
Malchus healed	Luke 22:51

The healings performed by Christ revealed many of His characteristics and His nature to provide healing for those that He created:

- A fulfillment of Christ's prophetic ministry (Isa. 53:4 and Matt. 8:16,17)
- An expression of Christ's compassion (Matt. 14:14; 20:34; Mark 1:40, 41; 5:19; 9:22)
- A conveyance of God's mercy (Phil. 2:17)
- Evidence that the Father sent Him (Acts 2:22)
- His mission to destroy the works of Satan (1 John 3:8; Acts 10:38; Heb. 2:14)
- The manifestation of the works of God (John 9:1-7)
- To manifest the glory of the LORD (John 11:40; Luke 13:10-17)

Every wounded person has to make a conscious decision seek the LORD for guidance through the healing process. James Richards writes, "The starting place for the pathway out of pain and into sanity is to always remind ourselves of the truth: We are accepted in Jesus and are righteous only in Him. We are free from every curse of the law because we are in Him. We are qualified for every aspect of the inheritance through Him. And every promise God has ever made to anyone is "yes" because we are in Him (2 Cor. 1:20)."[16] One of the promises that Richards speaks of is healing. As joint heirs with Christ, Christians have access to the promises of the King. This includes the healing virtues of Jehovah Rapha, our healer. Biblical evidence reveals the LORD's heart and yearning to heal those who have been wounded. The wounds of abuse and neglect can be confronted and conquered with the help of the LORD.

The Fallout

A term used to describe the aftereffects of military attacks is the word *fallout*, a term that describes "a secondary and often lingering effect, result, or set of consequences; whatever comes as an incidental consequence."[17] This definition is specifically related to nuclear attacks. Radioactive debris remains in the earth's atmosphere long after detonation. The radioactive material emits various ionizing radiations (i.e., gamma rays, alpha particles, electrons, etc.). This radiation can be fatal to those who come in close proximity.

A number of behavioral dysfunctions are associated with the fallout of child abuse and neglect. Without godly confrontation and healing, the after affects from this fallout can last for an extended period of time. Examples of fallout associated with child maltreatment are turbulent mood swings stemming from maltreatments and physical problems (such as heart problems and high blood pressure) which are directly linked to stress from the lasting memories of molestation. There are a host of other painful symptoms that are directly linked to the lingering effects of abuse and neglect.

In chapter 2, an analysis of the behavioral dynamics was included for each of the four major maltreatments affiliated with child maltreatment. The table on the next page is a brief synopsis of each of these dynamics.

Figure 7-4
Synopsis of Behavioral Dynamics[18]

Maltreatment	Behavioral Dynamics: Child
Neglect	Constant fatigue, listlessness, delayed speech, inappropriate seeking of attention, emotionally flat, pessimism, distrust, academic underachievement, delinquency, verbalizing that there is no caretaker in the home.
Physical Abuse	Aggressive behavior, withdrawal, fear of home, vacant or frozen stare, inappropriate or precocious maturity, poor self-concept, indiscriminately seeks attention, wary of adult contact, apprehensive when other children cry, feels deserving of punishment.
Sexual Abuse	Unwillingness to change clothing at gym class, poor peer relationships; unusual, bizarre, or sophisticated behavior or knowledge; infantile behavior; frequent delinquent or runaway; fantasizing or withdrawal from others; reports of sexual assault by caretaker.
Emotional Abuse	Certain habit disorders, biting or rocking back and forth, conduct or learning disorder, antisocial behavior, destructive behavior, sleep disorders, neurotic traits, inhibition of play, unusual fearfulness, behavioral extremes, overly compliant or passive, inappropriate adult or infantile behavior, developmental lags, mental or emotional problems, suicide attempts.

It has been discovered that several other behavioral dynamics are related to abuse and neglect. Some of these dynamics are illustrated in the following table.

Figure 7-5
Behavioral Traits Resulting From Child Maltreatment[19]

Anxiety	Depression	Feelings of Abandonment
Loneliness	Isolation	Rejection
Fear	Guilt	Lust
Anger	Judgmental Behavior	Lack of Acceptance
Lack of Support	Unmet Needs	Homosexual Lifestyle
Disintegrated Personalities	Shame	Guilt
Poor Relational Skills	Distrust	Poor Self Image

Though these lists are not exhaustive, they provide a framework that illustrates the emotional damage, or fallout, that lingers in individuals who suffered emotional trauma from the sinful acts of child maltreatment. Words of comfort are found in Romans 8:17. The passage declares: "and if children, then heirs—heirs of God and joint heirs with Christ, if indeed we suffer with Him, that we may also be glorified together." The passage gives Christians assurance that those who have endured suffering on earth are joint-heirs with Jesus Christ and have a promise from the LORD that they will be glorified with Him in heaven. The LORD is so gracious that being glorified with Him in heaven is only half of the equation. Not only do Christians have the promise of an eternal glorification in heaven, but can also experience divine healing here on earth.

The Healing Process

Understanding God's love and compassion is important for those who desire healing from past wounds. It has already been established that the evil that exists in the world is not from the LORD but is the result of sin. The negative influences that result from this sin distort the formation of human personalities. If not healed, the emotional damage caused by this distortion results in pain that can exist indefinitely.

Healing of child maltreatment occurs when there is a re-formation of distorted personalities, which empowers individuals to perceive themselves as God perceives them. Correcting a distorted self-image is essential in the healing process. Satan will continue to skew self-perceptions. The enemy's efforts will continue until the truth of God's Word is used to counter the distortion. The results of negative influences used by the adversary; namely, guilt, shame, embarrassment, low self-worth/poor self-esteem, anger, resentment, and unforgiveness are obvious. What is there to look forward to when the healing process begins? Those who have had their judgment clouded by child maltreatment can enjoy the simple pleasures of life that others may take for granted. They are given the opportunity to appreciate everything that God's world has to offer. Healing removes the pain and gives them the chance to live an abundant life.

The Development of a Distorted Self-Image

In chapter 3, we examined the enemy's efforts to pervert the biblical blueprint of godly relationships. The beginning of this rebellion occurred in Genesis 3 and continues today. Part of this perversion comes in the form of child maltreatment.

Scripture reveals the creative work of the LORD in Psalms 139:13-17:

> For You formed my inward parts; You covered me in my mother's womb. I will praise You, for I am fearfully and wonderfully made; marvelous are Your works, and that my soul knows very well. My frame was not hidden from You, when I was made in secret, and skillfully wrought in the lowest parts of the earth. Your eyes saw my substance, being yet unformed. And in Your book they all were written, the days fashioned for me,

when as yet there were none of them. How precious also are Your thoughts to me, O God! How great is the sum of them!

Psalms 139:13-17

Paul's words to the church at Ephesus describes God's creative efforts. "For we are His workmanship, created in Christ Jesus for good works, which God prepared beforehand that we should walk in them" (Eph. 2:10). The LORD ordained plans for every person. However, the influences of the world have had an adverse effect on many through a variety of experiences. These influences shape personalities and self-perceptions. If the distorted personalities and perceptions are not countered by Scripture and the Holy Spirit, the damage could last a lifetime.

When individuals experience maltreatment during their formative years, negative life experiences directly affect the development of their personality. The incidents can cause lasting memories that affect the way in which they develop. Distorted self-images are formed as a result of what people experience (e.g., abuse and neglect) that potentially hinder the formation of healthy relationships. These individuals are trapped in the fallout of the maltreatment and their ability to enjoy healthy relationships is affected by the experiences that they encountered as children.

Social surroundings that we are raised in also have a tremendous impact on the formation of personalities. There are myths associated with child maltreatment relative to social settings. Child maltreatment is not limited to poverty-stricken neighborhoods. The deceptive nature of the enemy would influence members of society to focus solely on these areas; however, the media regularly reports incidents of child maltreatment that occur across socioeconomic boundaries. The influences that shape the personalities of children visually or audibly in their environmental surroundings affect the way in which they view themselves and others. If reared in environments consisting of constant threats, neglect, or exploitation, children's personalities reflect the information communicated and retained in these environments. Negative social influences such as cultural preferences and traditions also have the potential to impact children in a manner that can produce pain and unwanted behavior. The child that is reared in an environment that neglects the proper care and nurturing of children will develop a non-biblical view of self-worth.

Chapter 3 explored the development of a child's cognitive processes. The study centered on the fallen nature of children (as well as adults who have not accepted Christ as Savior and LORD) who need specific instruction. What children are taught, either directly or indirectly, helps to establish their worldviews regarding their own self-worth, gender, race, ethnicity, and world systems. Worldviews are how people view the world based upon their biblical knowledge, or lack thereof. When children receive misinformation about discipline, sexuality, and self-worth, they form opinions based upon what they have been taught. These opinions become part of a complex system of untruths.

According to Matthew 25:15, each individual has been uniquely made by the LORD, with various abilities. "And to one he gave five talents, to another two, and to another one, to each according to his own ability; and immediately he went on a journey." Each individual is created with distinct gifts and personalities. F. D. Bruner comments, "In the kingdom of Christ not all are created equal."[20] Even with varying degrees of God-given abilities humans cannot maximize their God-given potential unless there is a total reliance on the Word of God and the Holy Spirit to provide healing from negative influences.

The chalkboard writings of lives distorted by child maltreatment have left painful memories hindering personalities from being fully developed. Satan, who, "is a liar and the father of it" (John 8:44), has deceived many individuals. He influenced them to believe the worst of themselves and others as a result of abuse and neglect. The way to effectively combat the enemy and continually work through the healing process is to allow the Holy Spirit to correct the distorted images within the mind, soul, and spirit. Cecil Osborne comments on the healing presence of God:

> The apostle Paul writes to the Christians at Philippi, "Have no anxiety about anything, but in everything by prayer and supplication with thanksgiving let your requests be made known to God. And the peace of God, which passes all understanding, will keep your hearts and minds in Christ Jesus." God's peace can come to us only as we surrender our anxiety and fear…Inner peace and harmony, the absence of destructive anxiety, provide the emotional climate in which our bodies can function best, and our lives develop creatively. This is attested to by the Bible and confirmed by the findings of modern science.[21]

As requests for healing are made known to God, they must be accompanied by releasing the painful memories of the past and turning them over to Him. By turning the pain over to the LORD and relying upon Him to provide healing, the abused or neglected individual acknowledges dependence upon Him. God not only honors this dependence, but relishes the opportunity to exhibit His healing virtues through the gracious compassion that He showers upon the individual.

Author Leanne Payne shares stories of people who could not live in victory because of the "diseased inner vision of themselves."[22] These inner visions come directly from the devil, for it is he that distorts proper self-images. The LORD counters this when there is total surrender of past hurts to Him and ultimate dependence upon Him for healing. Payne writes:

> Only the real "I," shedding its illusory selves, can draw near to God. In His Presence, my masks fall off, my false selves are

revealed...To continually abide in His presence is to have one face only–the true one. To draw near to Him, therefore, is to find the real "I" as well as its true home, my true center. Prior to this, I am split; I walk alongside myself, I am egocentric, I am uncentered.[23]

True healing occurs when individuals counter the lies that promote negative self-images. The *Truth*, Jesus ("I am the Truth" John 14:6) will set a person free. The understanding that abusive or neglectful experiences affect children's identities should motivate those who have the opportunity to positively influence children to help them in the development of an intimate relationship with the LORD. Children's lives are dependent upon this relationship.

Some have believed the lies of the devil concerning their self-image. Their behavior is evidence of the destructive influences. However, Scripture declares many truths regarding the identity of God's children. By adopting these truths, the traumatic incidents of the past no longer have power to induce negative self-images. Jesus declared in John 8:31-32, "If you abide in My word, you are My disciples indeed. And you shall know the truth, and the truth shall make you free." Healing and freedom from past wounds is attained with a knowledge of the gospel of Christ.

One of the most harmful devices of the enemy is his ability to influence people to cause harm to others. These harmful actions affect individuals in such a manner that they devalue themselves. David Seamands writes,

In a tape entitled "Satan's Psychological Warfare," Christian psychologist Jim Dobson tells about a poll he took among a large group of women. Most of them were married, in excellent health, and happy. According to their own statements, they had happy children and financial security. On the test Dr. Dobson listed ten sources of depression. He asked the women to number them in the order of how the ten affected their lives. This is the list he gave them:

- Absence of romantic love in your marriage,
- In-laws conflicts,
- Low self-esteem,
- Problems with children,
- Financial difficulties,
- Loneliness, isolation, boredom,
- Sexual problems in marriage,
- Health problems,
- Fatigue and time pressure,
- Aging.

The women rated these by the amount of depression each produced. What came out way ahead of all the others? Low self-esteem. Fifty percent of these Christian women rated it first; eighty percent of them rated it in the top two or three. Can you see the wasted emotional and spiritual potential? These women were battling depression, which came chiefly from the downward pull of the feelings of low self-worth.[24]

Many of the physical indicators and behavioral dynamics of child maltreatment are related to an improper view of self-esteem. The charts have illustrated that children develop insecure attachments, depression, and an erosion of self-esteem as a result of maltreatment. There is also the development of poor relational skills among peers. The report from Seamands suggests the overwhelming need to address the psychological damage that adults harbor. The data gathered by the *Department of Health and Human Services* suggests that there could be hundreds of thousands of adults that are carrying pain from past child maltreatment. These people are in need of the truth of God's Word to counter their improper view of self-worth.

Neil Anderson gives insight into the biblical identity of Christians in relation to Jesus Christ. These Scriptures will assist in countering the lies of Satan. Christians will be empowered through Scripture to be healed from the deceptive influences of the enemy when they embrace their true identity as born-again believers in Christ Jesus.

Figure 7-6
Every Believer is Identified With Christ[25]

In His Death	Romans 6:3, 6; Galatians 2:2, Colossians 3:1-3
In His Burial	Romans 6:4
In His Resurrection	Romans 6:5, 8, 11
In His Ascension	Ephesians 2:6
In His Life	Romans 6:10, 11
In His Power	Ephesians 1:19, 20
In His Inheritance	Romans 8:16, 17; Ephesians 1:11,12

Figure 7-7
Your Identity as a Christian in Christ[26]

I am the Salt of the Earth	Matthew 5:13
I am the Light of the World	Matthew 5:14
I am a Child of God	John 1:12
I am a Part of the True Vine, a Channel of Christ's Life	John 15:1, 5
I am Christ's Friend	John 15:15
I am Chosen and Appointed by Christ to Bear His Fruit	John 15:16
I am a Slave of Righteousness	Romans 6:18
I am a Son (or Daughter) of God; God is Spiritually My Father	Romans 8:14, 15; Galatians 3:26; 4:6
I am a Joint Heir with Christ, Sharing His Inheritance with Him	Romans 8:17
I am a temple-A Dwelling Place-of God. His Spirit & His Life Dwell in Me	1 Corinthians 3:16; 6:19
I am United to the Lord & am One Spirit With Him	1 Corinthians 6:17
I am a Member of Christ's Body	1 Corinthians 12:27; Ephesians 5:30
I am an Heir of God Since I am a Son (or Daughter) of God	Galatians 4:6,7
I am a Saint	1 Corinthians 1:2; Ephesians 1:1; Philippians 1:1; Colossians 1:2
I am God's Workmanship-His Handiwork-Born Anew in Christ to do His Work	Ephesians 2:10
I am a Fellow Citizen with the Rest of God's Family	Ephesians 2:19

Your Identity as a Christian in Christ (cont'd)	
I am Righteous & Holy	Ephesians 4:24
I am a Citizen of Heaven, Seated in Heaven Right Now	Ephesians 2:6; Philippians 3:20
I am Hidden with Christ in God	Colossians 3:3
I am an Expression of the Life of Christ Because He is My Life	Colossians 13:4
I am Chosen of God, Holy & Dearly Loved	Colossians 3:12; 1 Thessalonians 1:4
I am a Son (or Daughter) of Light & Not of Darkness	1 Thessalonians 5:5
I am a Partaker of Christ; I Share in His Life	Hebrews 3:14
I am a Holy Partaker of a Heavenly Calling	Hebrews 3:1
I am a Member of a Chosen Race, a Royal Priesthood, a Holy Nation, A People for God's Own Possession	1 Peter 2:9, 10
I am an Alien & Stranger to This World in Which I Temporarily Live	1 Peter 2:11
I am an Enemy of the Devil	1 Peter 5:8
I am a Child of God & I Will Resemble Christ When He Returns	1 John 3:1,2
I am Born of God, & the evil one-the devil-Cannot Touch Me	1 John 5:18
I am Not the Great "I AM"	Exodus 3:14; John 8:24; 28; 58
By the Grace of God, I am What I am	1 Corinthians 15:10

These passages reveal the true identity and personal characteristics of those who accept Christ as their Savior. The spiritual, emotional, and physical makeup of each Christian can be found within each of these Scriptures. No longer can the lies that influence negative personality or behavioral traits of child maltreatment cause pain. Once those who have been wronged gain an understanding of their true identity in Christ, there is a transition from victimization to healing. This transition may be a gradual process or it may occur instantly. Obstacles that harm healthy relationships, the fulfillment of dreams, and the materialization of personal vision are conquered as these truths are embraced. Those who have been harmed will begin to blossom into the man or woman God created them to be as the truth of God's Word becomes evident in their lives. Assistance by mature Christians is critical to this process.

Maximize Your Healing

A distinguishing component that sets apart biblical healing from the methodologies of secular therapists is the principle of forgiveness. Some secular counselors do not advocate forgiveness as a necessary principle of healing. Their focus is primarily on assisting their client to work through internal strife in their own strength–without addressing forgiveness. Individuals are instructed on the importance of confronting the pain and the offender, but seldom does the process include guidance to forgive. It is as though they believe that forgiveness will absolve the offender from the consequences of the harm that they caused. That view is not biblical. Scripture teaches that God is a God of justice and will repay those that do evil (see Romans 12:19, Deuteronomy 32:35, Isaiah 30:19, Isaiah 61:8). Gary Haugen writes:

> Amid a world of injustice, oppression and abuse, we can know some simple truths about God if we study his Word. No matter what the circumstances, we can depend on what he has revealed about himself. In regard to injustice our heavenly Father bids us to trust in four solid truths about his character.
>
> • God loves justice and, conversely, hates injustice.
> • God has compassion for those who suffer injustice–everywhere around the world, without distinction or favor.
> • God judges and condemns those who perpetrate injustice.
> • God seeks active rescue for the victims of injustice.[27]

Forgiveness helps to relieve those who have been harmed. As they embrace this biblical principle, the Holy Spirit begins working with them internally. Healing then, is the result of their obedience to Scripture. Forgiveness, coupled with resistance to cast judgment, allows the peace of God to facilitate healing in those who have been harmed. R. T. Kendall masterfully illustrates the importance of the biblical principle of forgiveness.

Total Forgiveness

One of the major hindrances that prevents forgiveness is the desire for vengeance. There are numerous examples in Scripture that illustrate the downward spiral resulting from a person seeking vengeance against an offender. A classic example of this is the demise of King Saul, who sought to kill David. He exhibited a spirit of hatred, revenge, and bitterness. This type of behavior can ruin the lives of those who have been offended and who do not release their pain through practicing a lifestyle of forgiveness.

R. T. Kendall describes his personal experience with unforgiveness and the difficult lessons he learned while embracing total forgiveness. The following paragraph summarizes the intensity of his journey.

> Most of us have times in our lives when we are pushed to our limits as to how much we are called to forgive. I remember what happened to me with such clarity. I have vowed not to retell this story, but suffice it to say I had never been hurt so deeply, before or since. The wrong I believe was done to me affected just about every area of my life: my family, my ministry, my very sense of self-worth. I felt at times like Job when he cried, "I have no peace, no quietness; I have no rest, but only turmoil" (Job 3:26); or like David when he prayed, "Answer me quickly, O LORD; my spirit fails. Do not hide your face from me or I will be like those who go down to the pit" (Ps. 143:7). I doubt that those who brought this situation upon me had any idea what I went through, and I pray they never will.[28]

Child abuse and neglect can result in the individual feeling like Kendall during those tumultuous times. The pain can become unbearable and the psychological fallout so enormous that words cannot begin to express what is felt internally. There must be an answer to this life of turmoil. The LORD should always be praised, because He provides healing through His Word, His presence in the form of the Holy Spirit, and through total forgiveness.

Kendall's friend from Romania, Josif Tson, gave him the best advice that a friend could give regarding feelings of resentment, anger, and pain as the result of being wronged by someone. Tson's advice to Kendall was, "R. T., you must totally forgive them. *Release them, and you will be released*" [emphasis added].[29] Tson understood a spiritual principle that does not receive an enormous amount of attention in the Christian community. The power of forgiveness is more than phenomenal; it is supernatural.

A significant principle of forgiveness is found in Mark 15:12-13. Christ is brought before Pilate and an angry crowd. When asked what sentence the crowd desired for the "King of the Jews" the crowd shouted "Crucify Him." After enduring pain and humiliation, along with having to bear the weight of the world's sin, Jesus responded with a simple, yet profound statement. In Luke 23:34, Christ asked the Father to, "...forgive them, for they do not know what they do." Christ illustrated a biblical principle that many Christians have failed to embrace. *Forgiveness benefits those who have been offended.* It also allows those who practice forgiveness the opportunity to move on with their lives and fulfill the destiny that God has for each individual. The prophet Jeremiah wrote in Jeremiah 29:11, "For I know the thoughts that I think toward you, says the LORD, thoughts of peace and not of evil, to give you a future and a hope." It is the LORD's desire to provide healing and fulfill His plan for a future and a hope for everyone who embraces Him. As forgiveness is practiced, the LORD's plan becomes clear and healing is activated.

Christ ascended into heaven and offered prayers of intercession for those that demanded His execution. He released the urge to become judgmental and angry toward those who crucified Him. If He had not, then He would not have accomplished the Father's will. Jesus understood the principle and benefits of total forgiveness.

Reciprocal forgiveness is also critical. Scripture teaches that forgiveness results in grace from our heavenly Father as He offers reciprocal forgiveness to those who have been offended. Luke 6:38 states, "Give, and it will be given to you: good measure, pressed down, shaken together, and running over will be put into your bosom. For with the same measure that you use, it will be measured back to you." This passage is often taken out of context as it is taught in relation to financial gain. But, Christ's intentions are clearly related to spiritual freedom through forgiveness. The surrounding passages support a reciprocal spirit of forgiveness from God the Father to those who forgive. This type of prosperity is far greater than any amount of economic wealth. It releases those who have been wronged from psychological bondage–an outcome that no amount of money can purchase.

> Mary, a friend of our family's, overcame painful memories of abuse in a similar way: My mother died at the age of forty-two, leaving behind my father and eight children, ages one through nineteen. This loss was devastating for our family, and my father broke down emotionally just when we needed him most. He tried to molest my sister and me, and so I began to resent his presence and hate him. He then moved away. I went off to school in Europe, and I didn't see him for another seven years. But I held on to my hatred and it grew inside of me. Later I returned to South America, where I became engaged to a childhood friend. At this point, my father asked me to meet him, but I refused. In no way did I want to meet him. My fiancé insisted. He said that I could not refuse such a meeting, and that I had to respond to his longing for reconciliation. It cost me a real battle,

but in the end I agreed, and we knelt down in prayer to ask for God's help. Peace came into my heart. We met my father in a café, and before I had said anything he turned to me, broken, and asked for my forgiveness. I was deeply moved, and I realized that to hold on to my hatred any longer would be a sin. I also saw that my anger had closed the door to God and His forgiveness and love in my own life.[30]

Unforgiveness vs. Forgiveness

There is a biblical standard that calls for Christians to live a lifestyle of forgiveness. This principle can be difficult to grasp, depending upon the nature of the offense. Scripture declares that believers continuously forgive so that they might be forgiven the offenses that they commit. When forgiveness is not practiced by Christians, they activate judgment against those who caused harm. James Richards describes an element of judgment: "when we assume to know why a person did what he did…we have entered into judgment."[31] Unforgiveness and judgment can produce personality flaws that attempt to "justify any negative or evil behavior we choose to act out. It is the pathway to personal idolatry. Our judgments, when imposed, cause people to bow to our wills."[32] Richards sights that when an individual judges because of being wronged, significance is attached to the traumatic event, thus planting the seeds of bondage. He shares a personal account of physical abuse that robbed him of joy for many years.

> I grew up in a rough and violent situation. I saw violence at a young age as my father physically abused my mother. At some point very early in my life, my father threatened to burn the house down with my family in it. I was around eleven years old the first time I was ever knocked out. My stepfather was beating my mother, and I stepped in to protect her. When I was eighteen years old, after being away from home for five years, I went back to spend a couple of nights and visit with my family. While

I was there, my stepfather attempted to kill me in my sleep.

Sometimes, when people hear parts of my testimony, they say, "I can't imagine how you can be even close to normal." They think that those circumstances should have had a greater abiding effect on my life. Although I do have emotional issues that I have not yet fully realized, the events that I have described have no real significance in my life today...Before I received Jesus as my Savior, I was very bitter and filled with hate for my stepfather. I thought of murdering him. After I was saved, I released him from my judgment and freed myself from the pain.[33]

Both Kendall and Richards share thoughtful insight of the powerful effect unforgiveness and judgment can have in the lives of those who have been wronged. Clinging to anger, bitterness, and resentment allows Satan the opportunity to negatively impact lives for years after the harmful incident occurred. As forgiveness is given, the pain from the past wrongdoing no longer has control or power in the life of the abused or neglected. The traumatic event no longer occupies a place of significance in their heart as they yield to the Holy Spirit who provides comfort for those wounds.

Forgiveness Does Not Absolve the Evil of the Wrongdoer

Forgiveness is not weakness, nor does it minimize the harm caused by others. Forgiveness, quite the contrary, is a sign of inner strength and an essential element of healing. Abuse and neglect should never be minimized and must be reported to the proper authorities. *There is another biblical principle that is woven throughout Scripture–sowing and reaping.* There are consequences for sin. Those who harm children should be reported to law enforcement officials. They should be held accountable by the judicial systems of the world. R. T. Kendall offers the following insight into what forgiveness does and does not entail.

What Total Forgiveness Is

- Being aware of what someone has done and still forgiving them
- Choosing to keep no records of wrong
- Refusing to punish [**see footnote**]
- Not telling what they did [**see footnote**]
- Being merciful
- Graciousness
- An inner condition
- An absence of bitterness
- Forgiving God
- Forgiving ourselves[34]

What Total Forgiveness Is Not

- Approval of what they did
- Excusing what they did
- Justifying what they did
- Pardoning what they did
- Reconciliation
- Denying what they did
- Blindness to what happened
- Forgetting
- Refusing to take the wrong seriously
- Pretending we are not hurt[35]

There are consequences for harming children, just as there are consequences for unforgiveness and judgment. As previously stated, no one should ever be exonerated for acts of evil. However, the deceptiveness of Satan is so subtle that traumatic events can control the lives of those who have been offended even after justice has

191

been served. This occurs when unforgiveness and judgment are present. Those who have been harmed are continually victimized by the devil if they do not forgive the perpetrator and go on with their lives. Individuals can take charge of their lives and receive healing through total forgiveness. The biblical character, Joseph, illustrates how the LORD can fulfill His purposes through the lives of those who forgive. Joseph had the opportunity to save the lives of many after forgiving several offenses. He forgave his brothers for selling him into slavery and forgave Potiphar's wife for falsely accusing him of rape. How many Josephs are there in the world who the LORD is waiting to empower? If they would only ask the Holy Spirit to help them release the pain from past wrongs by practicing forgiveness, healing would be available.

The only people able to accomplish the task of forgiveness are those who have pain anchored in their lives. The decision is this: are they willing to confront those wounds from the past that are hindering them from fulfilling their potential? Is there an internal desire to address the lies of the enemy that have caused feelings of hopelessness, shame, guilt, fear, or embarrassment? If they are willing to confront the pain and the lies of the enemy, the LORD is willing (just as He was with David and Joseph) to heal their wounds. God has proven in Scripture and in the lives of countless others that He will help His children confront the enemy and, by His Spirit, heal the scars from the past. The LORD will then usher the brokenhearted across the threshold of pain into a life of wholeness and victory.

The Role of the Church

If there is an area where Christian congregations, organizations, and believers can improve it is to increase the love, care, and efforts to provide safe, welcoming environments where the abused and neglected can recover. Christians should embrace the opportunity to be facilitators of healing as they introduce the hurting to the

King. Many believers have done little more than offer sporadic prayer when the subject is broached. Prayer must be used as a tremendous catalyst in the healing process. James 5:16 proclaims, "The effective, fervent prayer of a righteous man avails much." However, it seems as though for the most part, the Christian community has been dormant in taking an active role in the battle against child maltreatment. James Wilder discusses the need for additional support:

> In the middle of the debate about retrieved memories, preschoolers and therapists are some who were abused as children in horrible ways for religious purposes. Many of these cult survivors are trying to live as normal lives as possible. The problem for the survivors whose cults were organized as families, or whose whole families were in the cults, is that leaving the cult means a total loss of family–a loss most people cannot even begin to imagine. Their welfare depends on spiritual adoption into new families...When they attend church they rarely experience a sense of acceptance or even freedom to express the issues that trouble them.[36]

In efforts to assist those who have experienced abuse and neglect, the Christian congregation must embrace with open arms an unconditional love for those who are hurting. The body of Christ must become the spiritual family of the abused and neglected. The role of Christians will be discussed in more detail later.

Jesus Rose with Scars

In John's gospel there is a profound truth associated with the resurrection of our LORD that often goes unnoticed. John wrote:

> Now Thomas, called the Twin, one of the twelve, was not with them when Jesus came. The other disciples therefore said to him, "We have seen the Lord." So he said to them, "Unless I see in His hands the print of the nails, and put my finger into the print of the nails, and put my hand into His side, I will not

believe." And after eight days His disciples were again inside, and Thomas with them. Jesus came, the doors being shut, and stood in the midst, and said, "Peace to you!" Then He said to Thomas, "Reach your finger here, and look at My hands; and reach your hand here, and put it into My side. Do not be unbelieving, but believing." And Thomas answered and said to Him, "My Lord and my God!" Jesus said to him, "Thomas, because you have seen Me, you have believed. Blessed are those who have not seen and yet have believed."

John 20:24-29

When Christ rose from the dead, having conquered the adversary of our souls once and for all, He rose with the scars that were inflicted upon Him by His executioners. Jesus Christ's scars remained and provided evidence to non-believers that He truly had been resurrected after His death. These scars were a sign that He had been brutally tortured, scourged, and murdered out of godly love for His flock. His resurrection provides proof that healing, restoration, and the total redemption of man's soul is available and achievable even though physical or emotional scars may occasionally surface. Acts 1:9 and Acts 2:34-35 reveal that the LORD took His rightful position at the right hand of the Father, reaffirmed His identity as the King of kings, and allowed the Holy Spirit to provide comfort for all on earth who embrace His Word.

Like Ellen, mentioned in Chapter One, this glimmer of hope is available to all who believe. Like, our LORD, you can allow your scars to be a living testimony to others who may be experiencing similar pains. Your pain can be healed by the resurrecting power of Jesus Christ. Ellen made a decision to be healed. It is a personal choice that we all must make when faced with hardships and personal adversity. Do not let the enemy of your soul rob you of the joy that is rightfully yours as a child of the King. The words of the LORD counter the influences of your past pain:

An Unearthly Healing

The thief [Satan] does not come except to steal, and to kill, and to destroy. I have come that they [mankind] may have life, and that they may have it more abundantly.

John 10:10

Choose life!

[1] Uri Rueveni and Ross Speck, *Therapeutic Intervention: Healing Systems for Human Systems,* (New York, Human Sciences, 1982), 24.

[2] Raymond J. Corsini, and Danny Wedding, *Current Psychotherapies*, (Chicago, Ill., F. E. Peacock, 1995), 3.

[3] Ibid., 142.

[4] Duane P. Schultz and Sydney Ellen Schultz, *Theories of Personality*, (Belmont, CA, Wadsworth/Thomson Learning, 2001), 41-397.

[5] Craig Bloomberg, *The New American Commentary: Matthew* (Nashville, Tenn., Broadman Press, 1992), 254.

[6] *Diagnostic And Statistical Manual Of Mental Disorders,* 4th ed., (American Psychiatric Association, 1994), 424.

[7] Bessel A. Van Der Kolk, *Psychological Trauma* (American Psychiatric press, 1987), 115.

[8] *Webster's New Riverside Dictionary*, (Boston, New York, Houghton Mifflin Company), s.v. "denial."

[9] *Denial*, [http://www.nh-dwi.com/caip-202.htm], referenced 8 October 2006.

[10] Cecil Osborne, *"The Art of Understanding Yourself: An Invitation to Wholeness and to Life Itself!"* (Zondervan Publishing House, 1967), 105.

[11] Murray J. Harris, *The New International Greek Testament Commentary: The Second Epistle to the Corinthians*, (Grand Rapids, MI, Eerdmans, 2005), 430-434.

[12] Gary Haugen, *Good News About Injustice: A Witness of Courage In A Hurting World*, (Downers Grove, Ill., InterVarsity Press, 1999), 79.

[13] R. T. Kendall, *God Meant It For Good*, (Charlotte, NC, Morningstar, 1986), 15-16.

[14] Karel Beyer, [http://www.fundamentelbiblechurch.org/Feature/fbcfeat2.htm.], referenced 7 October 2006.

[15] Mike Flynn and Doug Gregg, *Inner Healing: A Handbook for Helping Yourself & Others* (Downers Grove, Ill., Intervarsity Press, 1993), 47.

[16] James B. Richards, *How To Stop The Pain* (Whitaker House, 2001), 15.

[17] *The Merriam-Webster Dictionary*, 1997, s.v. "fallout".

[18] *Source*: South Carolina Department of Social Services.

[19] *Source*: South Carolina Department of Social Services.

[20] F. D. Bruner, *Churchbook*, (Dallas, TX, Word), 902.

[21] Cecil Osborne, *The Art of Understanding Yourself: An Invitation to Wholeness and to Life Itself* (Grand Rapids, Michigan, Zondervan, 1967), 42-43.

[22] Leanne Payne, *The Healing Presence* (Grand Rapids, MI, Baker Books), 82.

[23] Ibid., 83.

[24] David A. Seamands, *Healing for Damaged Emotions* (Colorado Springs, CO., Cook Communications Ministries, 2002), 48-49.

[25] Neil T. Anderson, *Victory of Darkness: Realizing the Power of Your Identity In Christ* (Ventura, California, Regal Books, 1990) 45-46.

[26] Ibid.

[27] Gary Haugen, *Good News About Injustice*, (Downers Grove, Ill., Intervarsity Press, 1999), 69-70.

[28] R. T. Kendall, *Total Forgiveness* (Lake Mary, Fl., Charisma House, 2002), xx.

[29] Ibid, xxii.

[30] Johann Christoph Arnold, *Seventy Times Seven*, (Farmington, PA, Plough Publishing), 55-56.

[31] James Richards, *How To Stop the Pain* (Whitaker House, 2001), 21.

[32] Ibid., 58.

[33] R. T. Kendall, *Total Forgiveness*, 19-34.

Note: Kendall's text is not geared specifically towards child maltreatment. Therefore, as with all things, these principles must be taken in the context in which they were written. All incidents of abuse and neglect should be reported to Children's Services and/or law enforcement. Justice must be exacted by law enforcement and the judicial system for those who harm children.

[34] Ibid., 11-19.

[35] Ibid., 11-19.

[36] James E. Wilder, *The Red Dragon Cast Down: A Redemptive Approach To The Occult And Satanism* (Chosen Books, 1999), 23.

Chapter Eight
An Unbeatable Partnership

The prophet Jeremiah sent a message from Jerusalem to the elders of the exile, the priests, the prophets, and the remainder of those whom King Nebuchadnezzar had taken captive from Jerusalem and into Babylon. Jeremiah's letter records:

> Take wives and beget sons and daughters; and take wives for your sons and give your daughters to husbands, so that they may bear sons and daughters–that you may be increased there, and not diminished. And seek the peace of the city where I have caused you to be carried away captive, and pray to the LORD for it; for in its peace you will have peace.

Jeremiah 29:6-7

Taken captive in Jerusalem and put into exile in Babylon, the children of Israel were not separated from God. Even though they were suffering the consequences of their disobedience as the LORD allowed them to be taken captive, Israel remained God's chosen people. He maintained a desire to accomplish His purposes through them. The children of Israel were removed from Jerusalem and from the constant presence of the LORD through the temple. A cultural and spiritual shock impacted the people in exile.

From a spiritual perspective this was enormous. During that era normative Judaism provided access to the presence of the LORD by visiting the temple. They lamented as they no longer had the benefits of the LORD or His presence. Psalm 137 describes their laments:

By the rivers of Babylon, there we sat down, yea, we wept when we remembered Zion. We hung our harps upon the willows in the midst of it. For there those who carried us away captive asked of us a song, and those who plundered us requested mirth, saying, "Sing us one of the songs of Zion!" How shall we sing the LORD's song in a foreign land? If I forget you, O Jerusalem, let my right hand forget its skill! If I do not remember you, let my tongue cling to the roof of my mouth–if I do not exalt Jerusalem above my chief joy.

Psalms 137:1-6

They sorely missed the absence of God and His provision. In spite of their disobedience, the LORD had compassion upon them and desired to use them to rescue the city.

Jeremiah chose two men of very noble character, Elasah and Gemariah, to deliver God's Word to His people. The following outline of the letter found in Jeremiah 29 discloses the instructions of the LORD:

1. **Build Houses** (and live in them)–they were to establish homes in the middle of Babylon.
2. **Plant Gardens** (and live off of them)–this was a reminder to Jeremiah as the LORD spoke to him in Jeremiah 1:10–"See, I have this day set you over the nations and over the kingdoms, to root out and to pull down, to destroy and to throw down, to build and to plant."
3. **Take Wives**–the LORD expected them to build homes, plant gardens, and raise families, as He expected them to settle down in Babylon.

In essence, the LORD wanted to establish His presence in an ungodly city like Babylon as He sought the welfare of the city.

The Scripture states, "Seek the welfare of the city where I have sent you into exile, and pray to the LORD on its behalf; for in its welfare you will have welfare" (Jer. 29:7, NASB). The Hebrew word *shalom* is used for welfare in this passage. Some limit the interpretation of the word *shalom* to the meaning of welfare or peace. However, the word has a much broader meaning, which brings the LORD's desires into focus. *Shalom* means not only welfare and peace, but also "completeness, wholeness, health, safety, soundness, tranquility, prosperity, perfectness, fullness, rest, harmony, absence of agitation or discord."[1] This definition suggests that the LORD had more in mind than establishing just peace and welfare in the city. His presence would also bring about completeness to an ungodly people. He desired that believers infiltrate the city of Babylon and have such a positive impact upon the people that safety, soundness, tranquility, rest, and harmony would become the standard by which people lived.

The LORD still desires for Christians to seek the *shalom* of the city for all of its citizens, including children. No longer can the Christian community remain passive in efforts to combat child abuse and neglect.

In 1964, a young woman from Queens, Kitty Genovese, was stabbed to death in New York City as her assailant attacked her over three different times during a thirty-minute period. He sexually assaulted her and ultimately inflicted fatal stab wounds while her neighbors watched in horror from their windows. As horrific as this murder was, equally tragic is the fact that none of the thirty-eight neighbors that watched the attack from their windows attempted to rescue Genovese. They did not call for help, nor did they telephone police to report the crime. They simply watched the attack from the safety of their apartments. Former editor of the *New York Times*, Abe Rosenthal, offered his explanation for the apathy of those who watched. Rosenthal reported that the apathy exhibited by the neighbors who watched Genovese being attacked was the result of psychological survival. Rosenthal surmised that in a world where millions of people have enormous amounts of needs, urgencies, and other issues, the only way an individual can survive is to become what the musical group Pink Floyd coined as "comfortably numb."[2]

Could it possibly be that Christians have become so engrossed in the stresses of life that many have become comfortably numb instead of seeking justice and *shalom* for those in need of care? Members of the first church in the New Testament were exhorted in Acts 6 to care for those who were in need. The Hellenistic Jews complained to the native Hebrews that their widows were not adequately cared for in the daily serving of food. There was an emphasis placed upon embracing service as a part of one's Christian heritage in this passage. The Greek word *diakonia* is used by the writer of Acts for service to others. *Diakonia* implies the following, relative to service:

Figure 8-1
Defining Diakonia (Christian Service)[3]

Affirming the poor, the oppressed, and the marginalized as the center of Christian concern.
From a holistic perspective, the administration of everything: one's body, life, time, and land.
Faith put into action.
A go-between, an agent of change, and a servant
The essence of the church as a continuous and committed discipleship to Christ for the rebuilding of world community and re-creating the fallen world according to the plans of God.
Social service, mercy.
Any form of service to other human beings, any expression of love and concern for another.

An Unbeatable Partnership

One of the foundational tenets of the Christian church is sharing the love and compassion of Christ with others through diligent service. The LORD is calling the body of Christ to seek the *shalom* of the city in regard to child abuse and neglect. As Christians are activated in this effort, partnerships with those who are currently involved in the war against child maltreatment are vital to ensure success. In Jeremiah 29:11, the LORD declared, "For I know the thoughts that I think toward you, says the LORD, thoughts of peace and not of evil, to give you a future and a hope." The welfare for God's people is connected to the instructions given earlier in verse 7–to seek the welfare of the city. As the Christian community shares the love of Christ in an ungodly environment that has been inundated with child maltreatment, the presence of the LORD is established, and the people, land, and atmosphere can experience healing.

Why Community Partnerships

How then, do we deal with the enormity of the sin related to abuse and neglect? Seemingly, no one entity can effectively overcome those who have caused harm to children. There are numerous endeavors, publications, forums, and think tanks; yet, a collaborative effort between these well-meaning groups has not been established to strategically plan a course of action. It is imperative that there be a collective effort to provide safety for children. *Partnership South Carolina* reports, "…in this day when budgets are short and needs are great, working alone will not get the job done. This traditional viewpoint simply allows for overlapping of areas of responsibility, duplication of offered services, and a less-successful-than-desired use of funds. Even if there were abundant resources for the budgets of all serving agencies, working independently is not an appropriate way to serve. Partnership is required."[4]

A missing element for partnerships is the participation of the Christian community. Since Satan is the primary perpetrator of child maltreatment, then, the body of Christ should be the primary offensive weapon used against him. Scripture declares in Ephesians 6:10-12,

> Finally, my brethren, be strong in the LORD and in the power of His might. Put on the whole armor of God, that you may be able to stand against the wiles of the devil. For we do not wrestle against flesh and blood, but against principalities, against powers, against the rulers of the darkness of this age, against spiritual hosts of wickedness in the heavenly places.

Although humans are the vessels that are being used to harm children, they are not the primary source of harm. The primary source of harm to children is Satan, with his spiritual forces of wickedness (other fallen angels) positioned as the secondary tier of evil. It is crucial that Christian congregations, organizations, and individuals become actively involved in community partnership efforts in order to have success. If there is going to be *shalom* for the hurting community of children, then the body of Christ must get involved. Statistics gathered annually reveal that governmental agencies cannot be successful without assistance from the community.

From a historical perspective American governmental agencies have only recently begun to get involved in the welfare of children. It is stated in *Foundations of Partnership*,

> ...government in America had a very small role in assuring social welfare until the 1930's. This role, first set in place in the Great Depression, expanded in the 1960's and 70's. Most religious organizations, despite some notable successes in supporting schools and hospitals, generally assumed a rather narrow charitable role. Similarly, despite the historic high profile of groups such as the Salvation Army and the introduction of the "United Way" of funding these groups, nonprofit organizations had limited resources and were able to serve a few of the needs...In the public arena, changes in welfare and other laws

in the last decade required difficult transitions of vulnerable people in seeking personal independence. Those who failed to make these transitions under the guidelines of public agencies turned to the religious and nonprofit community organizations for help, bringing greater stress upon those agencies. The consequences of these shifts has been that all helping organizations have been forced to assume new duties.[5]

As these agencies assumed new duties, the quality of their services diminished and the people who were (and still are) in need of care continue to suffer. A continual flow of administrative changes, job layoffs, and budget cuts happen in many state organizations whose mission is to care for children. As these occur, families, children, and communities bear the brunt of the many changes in administrative vision and the downsizing of staff.

Wisdom can be gained from cartoonist Walt Kelly, who decades ago created the character Pogo. Through his characteristic style of humor and satire, Kelly attributed these words to Pogo, "we have met the enemy, and he is us."[6] This slogan can be applied to the lack of community involvement in combating child maltreatment.

For most of Western history we have believed that "moving on" is the nature of being human. If you don't like the neighbors, move on. If there is bad weather, move on. If someone pushes you around, move on! Whatever the unhappy, disgruntled, survival circumstance, move on. This was well and good so long as there was open and available territory and that territory was isolated or fertile enough to protect you from whatever it was that you were moving on from. Cross the ocean and there's a new world. Cross the mountains and there are the plains. Cross the plains and there is the West. If you keep on moving, you can leave all your troubles behind.

But then one day we looked at the picture of the earth, a globe hanging alone in black space in the photographs relayed back by cosmonauts and astronauts. Suddenly we were confronted with the truth: there is no place to move! We are one people on one planet.

It was then that Pogo's insight became clear. The enemy is us. The rich are us. The poor are us. The mentally ill are us. The fighters, the lovers, the governors, the builders, the teachers, the adapters, the religious community, the lawmakers, the law-breakers–all are us.

We still like to talk about "those people" as if doing so excuses us and protects us. But, as we know from the pictures from space and from an admission about our own lives, there is nowhere to go. Whatever the human condition is, good or ill, it affects us all. All of us live with the results of research in medical science. All of us live with the results of crime. All of us live with the results of the moral choices made by everyone else in society.[7]

Though Satan, other fallen angels, and human perpetrators of child maltreatment are rightfully blamed for harming children, public indifference through a lack of community involvement (as in the case of Ketty Genovese) is also at fault. *Partnership South Carolina*'s organizational task force has proposed eight philosophical tenets that all Christians should embrace.

Figure 8-2
Partnership South Carolina's Philosophical Tenets[8]

1. All human beings are made in God's image and thus possess a basic dignity which comes from God and which must be protected.
2. Human dignity is protected when human rights are respected.
3. People are not only sacred, but also social and called to be in a relationship with families and communities.
4. Those who are poor and vulnerable must have a special place not only in our hearts and minds, but also in our policies and deeds.
5. As a citizen, each person has a responsibility and a duty to be active in service to the community.
6. We are called to be responsible stewards of our God-given limited resources and together we must use these resources for the good and benefit of all people.

Figure 8-2 (cont'd)

7. We are called to recognize and respect the roles and responsibilities of public and private organizations–secular and religious.
8. We have a duty to call and challenge one another to service in meeting the needs of the least of us.

These philosophical tenets reflect many components found in Jeremiah 29. As we embrace Ephesians 6 and the advice of the cartoon character Pogo, we must seek creative ways to develop effective partnerships within all communities.

Separation of Church and State

Much has been made over the past several decades regarding the issue of "separation of church and state." There is a belief among many Christians and non-Christians alike that the church and government should remain separate at every level. Non-Christians maintain that the Christian church should not impose its' morals, ethics, or values upon the U.S. government or government agencies. Juxtaposed to this belief, Christians fear government will impose itself upon the church and seek to restrict what can be taught from the pulpit. Many have based their views upon the faulty teaching of American history that has skewed what the founding fathers of America penned in the Declaration of Independence and the Constitution. This has resulted in a lack of involvement by the body of Christ in our communities.

David Barton suggests that much of the confusion began to occur in the 1920's when a new type of American historian emerged focusing primarily on teaching American history from an economic perspective. Barton states,

> In the 20's, 30's, and 40's, a new type of historian emerged. Historians such as W.E. Woodward, Charles and Mary Beard, and Fairfax Downey came to the conclusion that the only thing that motivated people was money–so let's teach history that way. They started

writing a whole new series of text books that focused on the economic view of history [the economic view of the Declaration, the economic view of the Constitution, the economic view of the American people]. When you apply this paradigm in the American history, the result is that we now learn about "taxation without representation" only because it is an economic view. It ("taxation without representation) was not "the" issue, just one of 27 issues of grievances given in the Declaration.[9]

One of Barton's major concerns is that many in the Christian community have embraced the false interpretation of phrase coined as 'separation of church and state.' Barton further states,

> Especially true in the role of he church–of ministers and Christians in the civil arena. Strident voices both inside and outside of the Christian community asserts that Christians never have been involved in the civil arena and shouldn't be now. Many Christians have embraced this constricting mentality and have adopted a compartmentalized view that allows them to express their faith and value in church but segregates those same values and faith in the civil arena. The teachings of the Bible reject this compartmentalized approach to life and our history proves that for generations Christians embraced the proper viewpoint.
>
> Today we have an opportunity few others in our history have had. An opportunity to dramatically improve our culture and to be 'salt and light' in a number of strategic areas in the public square. Yet the church will miss this opportunity and we will fail future generations unless we change our thinking and our actions. To do this we must first understand the true historical and biblical role of Christians in the civil arena.[10]

Historical records reveal that there were approximately 250 founding fathers that had a substantial impact on upon the establishing of America. There were more than 50 that framed the Constitution and 90 that developed the Bill of Rights. Historical records reveal that approximately 95% of the founding fathers were Orthodox Christians that framed their beliefs and values from God's Word. Signers of the Declaration of Independence such as: John Witherspoon, John Hancock, Samuel Adams, Robert Paine, Francis Hopkinson, Richard Stockton, John Adams, Benjamin Rush, John Trumble, James Madison, Daniel Webster, and Charles Thompson (among many others) wrote of their faith in God and the need to establish America based upon Christian principles.

Some historians proclaim that Thomas Jefferson and Benjamin Franklin were non-Christians and based their beliefs upon secular values instead of the Word of God. The following exercise will illustrate their reliance upon the Christian faith in forming America.

Figure 8-3
Historical Perspective of the Founding Fathers of America[11]

- We've been trained to recognize the 2 least religious founding fathers, **Benjamin Franklin & Thomas Jefferson**. They (secular historians) have tried to spin history by picking just a few of the 250 founding fathers and proclaim that the beliefs of the majority of the founding fathers coincided with Franklin and Jefferson.
- **Benjamin Franklin** recommended Christianity in the public schools in Pennsylvania and he moved to increase church attendance across the state.
- He (Franklin) made one of the nations most forceful defenses of Christianity when attacked by **Thomas Payne** (author of The Age of Reason); Franklin sited numerous Bible verses to prove his point in the establishing chaplains & daily prayer at the Constitutional Conventions
- **Thomas Jefferson**; recommended the great seal of the U.S. depict a Bible story and include the word "God" in the national motto; Jefferson closed presidential documents with the statement–"in the year of our Lord Christ"–thus evoking Christ in governmental documents.
- **Thomas Jefferson** approved having church services in the U.S. Capital; Jefferson had the U.S. Marine Corps band serve as the worship band in the Capital.

Figure 8-3 (cont'd)

- 1803 **Thomas Jefferson** (president of the U.S.) sent missionaries to the Indians using Federal funds.
- The intent of **Jefferson's** letter on the 'separation of church & state' was to keep the government from stopping public religious activities.
- Historians today will take a few founding fathers to represent the entire 250; they will use **James Madison** (one of the very last things he did was to come out with a writing called the "Detached Memoranda"–where he renounced the installation of chaplains, prayer, fasting, etc.) to state that the founding fathers were non-Christians.
- **Madison** is a good guy in the secular mind because he denounces his religious efforts.
- People pull out the non-religious statements and embrace them as the 'total' truth of what these founding fathers believed.
- **Daniel Webster**–"History is God's providence in human affairs."

Figure 8-4
Religious Beliefs[12]

- **John Witherspoon** (1723-1794); ordained minister of the Gospel, several books of sermons, responsible for 2 American editions of the Bible including Americans very first family Bible (1791).
- **Charles Thompson**–the secretary of Congress, he and John Hancock were the only 2 founders to sign the first draft of the Declaration of Independence; founder of an American edition of the Bible, the first translation of the Greek Septuagint-which took Thompson 25 years to complete the translation-it is still considered one of the most scholarly American translations of the Bible.
- **John Hancock** (as a Governor)–one of two dozen prayer proclamations he did for his state–overtly calls on people to acknowledge Christ as Lord and Savior–he had people pray and fast that if someone does not know Christ as Lord and Savior that they would come to know Him.
- **John Trumble** (Governor)–need to take up collections for missionary societies.

- **Dr. Benjamin Rush**–Dr. Rush was one of the 3 most notable fathers (Franklin & Washington)–father of American Medicine–founded 5 colleges/including the first college for women–National Leader in the Abolition Movement–1791 he founded the Sunday School movement in American (First Day Society which grew into today's Sunday School)–started the first Bible Society in America–benefits (1) personal relationship with Christ (2) If every individual owned a Bible and would just study & obey it--would diminish social problems (crime, slavery, etc.)–"it is in living by the Bible that man becomes both humanized and civilized".
- **Rush** developed the first stereotype printing to print Bibles faster/mass produced Bibles.
- **Samuel Adams**–"I…rely upon the merits of Jesus Christ for a pardon of all my sins."
- **Robert Treat Paine**–"I am constrained to express my adoration of…the Author of my existence in full belief of…His forgiving mercy revealed to the world through Jesus Christ, through Whom I hope for never ending happiness in a future state.
- **Charles Carroll** (died in 1832 at age of 95)–last surviving founding father–"On the mercy of my Redeemer I rely for salvation and on His merits, not on any works that I've done in obedience to His precepts." (Bold Declaration)–was so committed to Christianity that he built and funded a Christian house of worship (statue in the Capital located in the east central hall).
- **Francis Hopkinson** (church music director & choir leader)–responsible for the earliest hymnals in America (1767) with 150 Psalms and set them all to music with the words and musical notes on the same page (one of the first of it's kind) so that we can sing the songs like King David did years ago.
- **Richard Stockton**–was captured and tortured by the British–his health never recovered when provisions were made for an exchange of prisoners–he penned his last will and testament–"I think it proper here not only to subscribe to the entire belief of the great and leading doctrines of the Christian religion, such as the being of God; the universal defection and depravity of human nature; the Divinity of the person and the completeness of the redemption purchased by the blessed Savior;…of Divine faith accompanied with an habitual virtuous life…but also,…to exhort and charge [my children] that the fear of God is the beginning of wisdom."
- **John Adam**s writes Benjamin Rush regarding the revelation that comes from the Holy Spirit.

*"Since we don't know history we tolerate
a level of secularism"*[13]
David Barton, historian

The statement, 'separation of church and state' does not exist either in the *Declaration of Independence* or the *Constitution.* It was penned in a letter written by Thomas Jefferson, who was not in the country at the time the founding documents were being crafted, *with the intent being to keep government from stopping religious activities.* The intent was not to prevent members of the Christian faith from participating in the civil arena. As a result of misunderstanding the faith of the founding fathers of America and the intentions of Jefferson's words penned in his letter many Evangelicals have embraced the faulty teaching.

Although many of the founding fathers of America were Christian, they made a drastic mistake by not following through with their demand to end slavery (as the aftermath continues to be felt by African-Americans today). Their intentions were to have a country based upon the God's Word with Christian involvement in every aspect of society. However, when the anti-slavery laws that were passed in America were vetoed by the British government, it arguably began the most disastrous error in the history of the United States.

The Word of God and the involvement of the Christian community in the public arena is both biblical (Jeremiah 29) and at the core of the foundational documents of the United States of America. History confirms that 'forced/legislated' religion (i.e., the Crusades) does little to accomplish the will of God and can have devastating consequences. However, Christians must become involved in the fight against child maltreatment through the building of effective partnerships with stakeholders within our society if there is to be a reduction in the frequency of abuse and neglect in both our local and global communities.

The Foundations of Effective Community Partnerships

One of the best methods of establishing a vision for what community partnerships should entail is to determine what elements could potentially serve as hindrances to effective partnerships. The following list serves as potential pitfalls to developing strong community partnerships.

Figure 8-5
Hindrances to Successful Partnerships[14]

• Partnerships are not simply getting individuals or agencies together to accomplish what you have already decided needs to be accomplished in the way that you have determined.
• Partnerships are not used solely as opportunities to evangelize the lost.
• Partnerships are not opportunities to make other agencies, organizations, or individuals change into what you feel they should have been all along.
• Partnerships are not created for any one person or agency to be in charge.
• Partnerships are not designed for any one entity or individual to receive all of the glory.
• Partnerships are not for the sole purpose of a mutual exchange of resources.
• Partnerships are not effective when issues of turf/territory, motivation, poor communication, organizational structure, and evaluation, supercede the common goal.

The most effective manner of partnership development is to involve everyone in strategic planning, analysis, implementation, and evaluation of purpose. The objective(s) of the partnership, as well as the management of tasks, should be clear and concise. Each member of the partnership should receive an appropriate amount of recognition for individual successes brought to the partnership. To establish effective community partnerships for combating child abuse and neglect, the following suggestions from "Child Protection: Building Community Partnerships" are offered by Frank Farrow.

Figure 8-6
Establishing Successful Community Partnerships[15]

• Establish each community's goals for child protection.
• Design a neighborhood system of service delivery (a combination of natural helping networks and formal service providers that will assure children's safety).
• Work with all state and local public and private resources to assure that the delivery system for child protection has adequate funding.
• Engage the broader community (parents, the business sector, media, law enforcement, and others in the mission of child safety).
• Track the performance of the community's delivery system for protecting children and disseminating information so that the public is aware of the degree to which children are not safe.

By embracing the components of figure 8-4, community partners can create a safe environment (a place of rest) for children. Ultimately, an effective community partnership is defined as: "an alliance of peers with strengths and limitations, working cooperatively and interdependently toward a shared purpose."[16] One example of a community partnership is the *St. Louis Emerging Community Partnership.*

St. Louis's effort to change child protective services began as part of Missouri's implementation of "dual track" legislation. The Sigel Elementary School is building on that starting point to engage parents, child care providers, community agencies, and neighborhood organizations to form a community partnership for child protection (CPCP).

After nine months of working together, the partnership is still growing. A small core group consisting of the CPS agency director, the school principal, and several additional agency directors has expanded month by month, and every meeting of the partnership brings new members. Parents have been present since the second meeting and play a central role in planning and decision making.

This growth has many implications for the partnership's development. New participants must constantly be brought "up to speed." People accustomed to making decisions by themselves must modify their behavior. Most of all, however, their [sic] ever-widening circle means that the partnership's representation and engagement of the community becomes steadily stronger.[17]

The *St. Louis Emerging Community Partnership* is an example of potential partnerships in the community. However, note that no Christian organizations were mentioned (not that there are none involved at the present time). Jeremiah 29 implies that Christians are to be proactive in leading efforts to impact culture and community. Christians are not to merely react against those who do not share the same moral and ethical beliefs that are found in Scripture. The following are ways in which Christians can impact culture and community by becoming active participants in community partnerships.

What Role Can Christians Play in Community Partnerships?

The importance of Christian involvement in communities is evident. Christians assist in establishing biblical morals and ethics in society when they partner with others to achieve specific goals. They provide wisdom and discernment given by the LORD (1 Kings 3) as strategic decisions are made that pertain to goals of the community partnerships. There are several defined areas of involvement in which Christians play a pivotal role in partnerships.

Facilitation & Assessment: The first role of Christians is to have a discerning heart regarding the needs of their communities relative to child safety. In order to properly assess the needs, a community partnership needs to be established. This can be accomplished by contacting the local *Child Protective Service* agency to determine whether a community partnership exists. If one exists, Christians can volunteer to serve on the committee. If one does not, take the lead in developing a community partnership and invite the following organizations to participate: *Child Protective Service* agencies, law enforcement, group homes, foster homes, school personnel, etc. As the community task force or partnership is developed, Christians can structure guidelines based upon information provided in Figures 8-1 through 8-4.

Prayer: Christian volunteers have the ability to provide community partnerships with one of the most powerful and effective components necessary to combat child maltreatment–prayer. The core issues of child maltreatment are spiritual in nature (Eph. 6:12). In order to effectively engage those elements listed in Ephesians 6:12 (against principalities, against powers, against the rulers of the darkness of this age, against spiritual hosts of wickedness in heavenly places), there must be action that is proactive as well as reactive. Establishing prayer teams within local congregations is vital to the success of community partnerships whose mission is centered on defeating child maltreatment. The disciple James provides a spiritual truth in James 5:16 that is vastly ignored in the arena of child maltreatment: "Confess your trespasses to one another, and pray for one another, that you may be healed. The effective, fervent prayer of a righteous man avails much." Regardless of what the members of the community partnership develop as an agenda, prayer ensures its effectiveness. Prayer is of utmost importance because it communicates to the LORD a dependence and trust in Him to provide safety and healing for His children. As prayer teams are established within congregations, it is important that the teams be organized to allow for maximum effectiveness. James Wilder suggests the following:

> Care for the Prayer Ministry–Whatever the purpose of the team, it is important to avoid confusion by having one person in charge. For intercession of prayer support, the team can consist of many people. Though the leader guides the session, the usual

process allows individuals to lead as they feel prompted by the Holy Spirit...It is important to give opportunity for input from the members of the team. One approach that allows everyone to participate in a nonintrusive way is to have team members write down on slips of paper any insights that come to them during the session...Intercessors are those gifted in tackling a problem with tenacity, as Abraham did when he begged God to refrain from destroying Sodom (see Genesis 18:20-33).

Care of the Prayer Team–An important function of any ministry team, whether focused on healing or prayer, is providing an example to those in need. First, those responsible for ministry should be exemplary in their Christian walk. They should model compassion to those in need and teach others how to minister by their example...God attends to those who do the ministry...Ministry teams receive blessing beyond measure through constant involvement in doing things they know they cannot do, unless the Holy Spirit is there to provide the insight and power...The fact that we cannot do such ministry without the Holy Spirit teaches us that we dare not become proud of our own abilities.

Care of the Recipient–Ministry is guided by three factors: Scripture, the Holy Spirit and loving relationships. Intercessors can be especially helpful to those on healing teams by focusing their prayers on areas of a recipient's weakness...Often God gives encouraging words and Scriptures to these prayers to be passed along to other participants...They experience themselves differently when soaked in prayer in the presence of God...The wounded need both healing and support...It is the joint effort between the various team members, the community and the Holy Spirit to bring the recipient to freedom and a new course for life.[18]

Another emphasis of prayer can be praying against particular maltreatments that occur in specific zip codes in communities. Local social service agencies gather statistics regarding maltreatments that occur in certain geographical areas (i.e., incestuous relationships in isolated areas, physical abuse and neglect in areas known for drug abuse, etc.). This type of information can be taken to the LORD in prayer for His divine intervention.

Other prayer requests may include prayer for: legislators who determine laws and budgets, caseworkers, perpetrators (who are in need of salvation and/or restoration), public awareness and involvement, strategies to combat the sin issue, both national and international accountability, and the LORD's presence for protection of His children.

Adoption/Foster Care/Respite Homes: A vital role that Christians play in bringing *shalom* to the community is that of adoptive parents, foster parents, or respite providers (temporary shelters) for children who have been abused or neglected. Statistics from the *Administration for Children and Families* reveal that as of 2005 there were 513,000 children in care (custody) that were waiting to be reunited with their biological families or awaiting adoptive or foster care placement.[19] There are couples who have not been able to conceive and have adopted children either from biological parents or out of foster care. Testimonies reveal the joy parents found with the children who they have adopted. The LORD has richly blessed their lives because of the decision they made to help His children.

There are foster parents who periodically need to rest for a short period of time. They need a safe environment where they can entrust the care of their foster children. These safe places of rest are called respite homes. Christians can provide these temporary shelters to help children who have gone through numerous placements and have no sense of permanency or stability in their lives. These are excellent opportunities to share the love of Christ with a child.

Spiritual Adoption: James Wilder defines spiritual adoption as an effort by Christians to commit to working with those whom Satan has wounded. He describes the importance as it relates to those who have been abused by satanic cults:

> Once ex-pagans or ex-cult members and victims become part of
> the family of God, we are obligated as the Church to enable
> them to prosper by providing for those aspects of life that
> require a family's help. Ronda Perry describes in her book, *A
> Community of Healing*, how five couples in a Bible study group
> accomplished this. Such care is not always comfortable, nor
> does it appear safe from a human perspective. In fact, it can get
> quite messy at times and draw significant criticism from those
> who believe that where God is at work, things always go well.
> Still, John the elder and apostle reminds us that if we see a
> brother or sister in need and do not provide for them, then the
> love of the Father is not in us[20] (see 1 John 3:17).

A missing component in many Christian congregations, organizations, and individuals is that of unconditional love for the wounded. As people become familiar with one another in church settings,
they begin to form groups or cliques that are difficult for visitors to
penetrate. It is even more difficult for the wounded to find an environment where they do not feel threatened. Spiritual adoptions rarely
take place by cliques. The wounded never feel the love of Christ and
eventually seek acceptance from anyone who is willing to listen.
Wilder reports that young adults who have been victimized need
three elements for recovery: *relationships*, *power*, and *truth*.[21]
Relationships are needed to help form a new identity in Christ.
Power is needed to be effectively transformed in Christ-likeness
(Rom. 12:1-2). *Truth* of the gospel of Jesus Christ and that of their
own identity in Christ (see chapter 5) is needed to combat the lies of
Satan. Many churches and Christians practice religion without the
power of Christ. Wounded people need the power and truth of the
gospel as well as relationships with mature Christians who can assist
them by providing spiritual discipleship. This cannot be accomplished until churches, parachurch organizations, and Christians pro-

vide a loving environment for those who need to be introduced to the King.

Monitoring/Accountability/Development: Christians should hold agencies accountable for providing excellent service to children and families. These agencies have been entrusted with the lives of those that cannot adequately care for themselves. Someone must hold them accountable.

Administrations within local governments, social service agencies, law enforcement, group homes, foster care agencies, and therapeutic placements change regularly. Often, each new administration will result in a new agenda and area of emphasis. Changes in philosophy, methodology, service delivery, staff reduction and roles, as well as the allocation of resources demoralize staff and result in high turnover in departments. The end result is a lack of quality service provided to children and their families. Christians need to play an active role in monitoring what is occurring in these agencies. Legislators, agency directors, and other public officials are in need of prayer and must become a part of the community partnership to ensure that the best services possible are being provided for children and families.

Conclusion

Psalm 12:5 declares, "For the oppression of the poor, for the sighing of the needy, now I will arise," says the LORD; "I will set him in the safety for which he yearns." Since the days when children were being sacrificed to the false god Molech, the LORD has longed for those who believe in Him to partner with Him in providing a place of safety for all children. History has proven that children have been abused and neglected since the fall of man. Advocates such as the early pioneers of children's services, and present day caseworkers, have recognized the need to be a voice for those who have been ignored. History also bears witness to the fact that not much has changed in human behavior in relation to the maltreatment of children. The number of children known to have been harmed each year continues to hover close to the 1,000,000 mark in America alone.

There is no single entity that can adequately address the issue of child abuse and neglect. The necessary tenacity, resources, wisdom, and foresight needed to eradicate this sin are desperately needed. Through the collaborative efforts of community partnerships in America and abroad, the perpetrators of child maltreatment will be brought to justice and children will have the opportunity to grow up in safe environments. Children need a safe environment to become what the LORD desires.

The body of Christ can no longer expect those who are considered to be worldly or secular to lead the way in this effort. Christ is the answer relative to salvation for those who have been abused and neglected and for those who have caused the abuse and neglect. Christ and His body of believers are also a major part of the solution to prevention, identification, and healing. As we prayerfully consider what role we play as individuals, congregations, and Christian organizations, let us not forget the authority that Christ spoke of when He gave the Great Commission:

> And Jesus came and spoke to them, saying, "All authority has been given to Me in heaven and on earth. Go therefore and make disciples of all the nations, baptizing them in the name of the Father and of the Son and of the Holy Spirit, teaching them to observe all things that I have commanded you; and lo, I am with you always, even to the end of the age." Amen."

> Matthew 28:18-20

Making disciples of Christ and instructing them to observe all that He commanded is the role of Christians. Christ's earthly ministry included caring for children. Mark 10:13-16 illustrates how much Jesus loves and cares for children:

Then they brought little children to Him, that He might touch them; but <u>the disciples rebuked those</u> who brought them. But <u>when Jesus saw it, He was greatly displeased</u> and said to them, "<u>Let the little children come to Me</u>, and <u>do not forbid them</u>; for of such is the kingdom of God. Assuredly, I say to you, whoever does not receive the kingdom of God as a little child will by no means enter it." And <u>He took them up in His arms</u>, <u>laid His hands on them, and blessed them</u>." (emphasis added)

Mark 10:13-16

Christ's love for children is evident in this passage. This theme regarding children runs through the Scriptures. The LORD loves, cares for, and desires safe environments for all children. He expects Christians to play a major role in the efforts to ensure that child abuse and neglect is prevented when possible, identified when not possible, and to bring the wounded to Him for healing. The mandate for Christian involvement is clear and concise. We must get involved by loving others and providing justice through the body of Christ. We should actively seek Him to guide us into action as we continually petition Him in prayer:

Lord, Please Protect the Children and Continue Drying
the Silent Tears of Your Children.

220

[1] David Silver, *The Meaning of the Word Shalom*, [http://www.therefinersfire.org/meaning_of_shalom.htm], November 3, 2006.

[2] A. M. Rosenthal, *Thirty-Eight Witnesses: The Kitty Genovese Case*, (Berkeley, CA, University of California Press, 1999), 50-65.

[3] World Council of Churches, [http://www.wcc-coe.org/wcc/what/regional/comas.html], referenced 3 November 2006.

[4] *Partnership South Carolina's Guide to Successful Collaboration: Foundations of Partnership*, March, 2002, 3.

[5] Ibid., 3.

[6] *The Best of Pogo*, (NY, New York, Simon & Schuster, 1982), [http://www.igopogo.com/final_authority.htm], referenced 4 November 2006.

[7] Ibid., 5.

[8] Partnership South Carolina, *Foundations of Partnership*, 8.

[9] *The American Heritage Series* with Historian David Barton, DVD (wall-builders.com, 2007).

[10] Ibid.

[11] Ibid.

[12] Ibid.

[13] Ibid.

[14] Partnership South Carolina, *Foundations of Partnership*,12-14.

[15] Frank Farrow, *Child Protection: Building Community Partnerships*, (The President and Fellows of Harvard University, 1997), 44.

[16] Partnership South Carolina's *Guide to Successful Collaboration: Foundations of Partnership*, 10.

[17] Frank Farrow, *Child Protection*, 20.

[18] James Wilder, *The Red Dragon Cast Down*, 318-320.

[19] *Trends in Foster Care and Adoption*–FY 2000–FY 2005, [http://www.acf.hhs.gov/programs/cb/stats_research/afcars/trends.htm], referenced 8 November 2006.

[20] James Wilder, *The Red Dragon Cast Down*, 277.

[21] Ibid, 71.